HEAVENLY CAVES

REFLECTIONS ON THE GARDEN GROTTO

The greatest treasures and most wonderful things lie hidden underground — and not without reason.

Rabelais, *Gargantua and Pantagruel,* 5.48

HEAVENLY CAVES

REFLECTIONS ON THE GARDEN GROTTO

NAOMI MILLER

GEORGE BRAZILLER   NEW YORK

World Landscape Art & Architecture Series

General Editor
William Howard Adams

For information address the publisher:
George Braziller, Inc.
One Park Avenue
New York, NY 10016

Library of Congress Cataloging in Publication Data

Miller, Naomi.
   Heavenly caves.

   Bibliography: p.
   Includes index.
   1. Cave architecture.   2. Symbolism in
architecture.   3. Garden structures.
I. Title.
NA8455.M55   728'.9   81-18159
ISBN 0-8076-0966-8   AACR2
ISBN 0-8076-0967-6 (pbk.)

Front cover photo: Queen's Dairy, Rambouillet, © SPADEM,
Paris/VAGA, New York, 1982
Back cover photo: *Le Désert de Retz,* Grotto-rock viewed from
the garden entry through the Forest of Mary, ca. 1774.
Engraving from G.L. Le Rouge, *Nouveaux Jardins* . . . , cahier
XIII, Paris 1785. Photo courtesy of The Dumbarton Oaks
Research Library and Collection, Washington, D.C.

Book Design by Peter McKenzie

Printed in the United States of America
First Edition

TABLE OF CONTENTS

ACKNOWLEDGMENTS

> And after having remained at the entry some time, two contrary emotions arose in me, fear and desire — fear of the threatening dark grotto, desire to see whether there were any marvelous thing within it.
> Leonardo da Vinci, *Codex Arundel,* 155r⁰

At last I understand why I have never been able to find a single work devoted exclusively to garden grottoes. It is a topic whose sources and ramifications are infinite and "fools rush in where angels fear to tread." Many of Pope's contemporaries would have agreed with these words, especially when thinking of Pope's own grotto. The grotto is often a poetic work, and perhaps only a poet is fit to describe such. This said, I hope that the following introduction to the garden grotto may provide the inspiration for others to explore the theme and to penetrate beyond form to meaning.

My interest in the subject stems initially from a chapter, "The Fountain in the Grotto," in my dissertation, "French Renaissance Fountains." No work served more as a foundation for this study than Leonardo's words, cited above, upon confrontation with the grotto; just as important was André Chastel's marvelous exposition of this passage in conjunction with Plato's allegory in *The Republic* in *L'Art et humanisme à Florence au temps de Laurent le Magnifique,* Paris, 1959.

To many friends, colleagues, and institutions, I should like to express my gratitude: above all, to the Trustees of Dumbarton Oaks for the unparalleled opportunity to investigate the grottoes of sixteenth- and seventeenth-century France as a Senior Fellow in Landscape Architecture, 1976 to 1977. Dr. Elizabeth MacDougall, Director of the Garden Library, provided all possible encouragement, while Laura Byers and the staff added much pleasure to their welcome assistance. I should also like to express sincere appreciation to the following institutions where I had the privilege to study: the libraries of Harvard University; the Folger Library and the Library of Congress, Washington, D.C.; the Warburg Institute and the British Museum, London; the Bibliotheca Hertziana, Rome; the Avery Library, Columbia University, and the New York Public Library; and the Library of the Hebrew University of Jerusalem, where the writing was completed. To Boston University, my thanks for the leaves of absence to pursue this work.

Friends and colleagues have been incredibly generous and patient — and critical and severe — in reading parts or all of this manuscript. My deepest thanks to Professors David Coffin, Fred Kleiner, Fred Licht, James O'Gorman, Susan Staves, Owen Thomas, and above all to Donald Stone. An immeasurable debt is due to W. Howard Adams, whose suggestions and sustaining interest went beyond the bounds of editorship of this series, and to Patrick and Jacqueline Morreau, Elizabeth Moynihan, and Professor Colin Eisler, who provided continued support. In no way are any of these persons responsible for the final shape of this manuscript. The work remains, alas, in progress — like its subject, a place of passage.

Boston University
August 1980

I. INTRODUCTION: TRANSFORMATIONS OF A CLASSICAL THEME

> Above, too, is a background of shimmering woods with an overhanging grove, black with gloomy shade. Under the brow of the fronting cliff is a cave of hanging rocks; within are fresh waters and seats in the living stone, a haunt of Nymphs.
>
> Virgil, *Aeneid* 1.164-66

These chapters focus on a singular architectural topos — the grotto. A particular feature of landscape and garden, the grotto is a commonplace ubiquitous in antiquity and prevalent in classical sources. The revival and transformation of this motif are especially marked in Renaissance pastoral poetry and in humanist gardens. Because the grotto may be viewed in a myriad of contexts — sacred and profane, idyllic and bucolic, mythological and oracular, theatrical and ornamental — it constitutes an elusive art form. A relatively immutable element in the ephemeral world of the garden — a place of repose and reunion, or of solitude, seclusion, and shade; a site of assemblages for learned discourse; a museum and a triclinium; a sanctuary of muses and an abode of nymphs; a locus of enlightenment and poetic inspiration; a harbor for springs and fountains — the grotto is, above all, a metaphor of the cosmos. Variety of forms is almost as vast as variety of functions, with nature versus art as the leitmotif.

Yet despite the popularity of the grotto and the enormity of the relevant literature, no single work treats this architectural entity within a broad temporal spectrum. This particular study discusses the grotto as a classical conceit and its changing aspects as a result of changes in cultural conditions, in politics and patronage, and in attitudes toward nature. Any commonplace that is a metaphor for the cosmos must by its very nature be vague and lacking in definition. Hence the range of "types" here presented may seem inordinately wide and critical monuments are missing — for example, we have not discussed the spectacular grottoes in the Castle of Rosendael in the Netherlands, those in the Palace of Fronteira near Lisbon, and scores throughout Italy. Emphasis will be placed on those grottoes that are most

1. Castellana. Grotto.

allied to "rustic fountains," that is, to fountains designed for naturalistic settings rather than for architectonic ones. The presence of water — actual or implied — is the *sine qua non* of the garden grotto as of the fountain.

First, let us turn to the word itself. The English "grotto" is derived from the Latin *crypta* (from the Greek κρύπνη — vault or κρυπγείνω — to hide; as also from the Italian *grotta,* or French *grotte*), meaning a concealed subterranean passage, a vault, cavern, cave, grotto, or pit. The primary distinction in English, as in the Romance languages, is between a natural covered opening in the earth and an artificial man-made recess that resembles a natural grotto.

2. Florence, Boboli Gardens. Grotto, 1583–1593, B. Buontalenti.

8

3. Hadrian's Villa near Tivoli. Cryptoporticus, 2nd century A.D.

Further linguistic subtleties are encountered, as in the French distinction among *antre*, *caverne*, and *grotte*. In Huguet's sixteenth-century French dictionary, we find the word grotto under *crote* defined as *grotte, caverne*, and *crypte*, the latter referring to a *cryptoporticus*; it also appears under *grotesque* defined as an underground place, or capricious ornament. Speculation about the origin of *crote* leads to seductive possibilities of a connection with Croton, sometimes noted as the birthplace of Pythagoras and the site of his museum.[1]

The Latin *crypta* provides further ties to *cryptoporticus*, a subterranean portico. Pliny the Elder describes these as a means of communication between buildings in both his Laurentium and Tusculum villas. These villas were hypothetically reconstructed by Félibien in 1699 and by Castell in 1728.[2] The latter's description of the cryptoportici in the villas of Pliny and Cicero defines the structure as " 'an invention'... not in Vitruvius... a long room... a Porticus enclosed by a wall on all sides.... This room Pliny has here considered under three separate heads: first, its size; secondly, its contrivance to admit or exclude the wind and light at pleasure; and lastly, with respect to the heat of the sun both in summer and winter."[3] The many cryptoportici in Hadrian's villa provided passageways to avoid the heat of the day. This form is revived in the Renaissance, but its function is often quite different. For example, the cryptoporticus in the Château of Anet, built beneath the building on the garden side, serves both to lend support to its foundation and to give access to the garden.[4]

9

4. Château of Anet. Cryptoporticus, 1548–1552, P. Delorme.

Grottoes, especially in the sixteenth century, have been associated with the grotesque, the Italian *grottesca,* "a kinde of rugged unpolished painters worke, anticke worke."[5] *Grotte* became the popular Roman name for the underground vaults of ancient buildings revealed by such excavations as that of Nero's Golden House. They were adorned with mural decorations and capricious ornament known as *grottesche* — a fantastic intermingling of human, and animal, floral, and abstract forms, often framed in stucco medallions adhering to rigid geometric patterns. This type of decor later became a feature of Renaissance villas.[6]

Gombrich compellingly explains the Renaissance usage of "grotesques" and their source in Horace's *Ars Poetica,* where it is granted that "the artist like the poet can make use of make-believe" (but within the observance of decorum). To show the fashion of the grotesque *all'antica,* Gombrich presents a print by the Master of the Die, accompanied by a poem, attributing the source to Rome: "Whence now from grottoes where no people live/ So much new light on this fine art is spreading."[7] The unknown author of these verses is surely aware of Horace's lines concerning the license inherent in artistic creation.

To focus on the garden grotto is to focus on the artificial cavern — the creation of a cosmos in miniature, a nature that is cultivated and controlled. And if the classical grotto is so closely related to the natural source or spring as to be at one with it, time soon transforms it into an elaborate architectural conceit. Art imitating and surpassing nature: the theme is constant from Pliny to Palissy to Pope. New ideas about the universe and the forces that govern it are reflected in garden design. In some way the grotto is a reduction of the garden, partaking of all its characteristics. It, too, is a place for delight and meditation, for rest and recreation, for the restoration and renewal of the

10

senses, for private and public pleasures, for feasting and fooleries. Like the garden, the grotto may be an escape from the world of reality, from the rules and artifices and constrictions of society–and like the garden, the grotto may impose its own limits . Withdrawal into this illusory realm, into this world of fantasy, implies a communion, not with the outside world of nature still dominant in the garden, but here within the enclosed orbit of the grotto with the inner world of man.

Contemplation and creation constitute the higher forces, the Apollonian side of the grotto. But in a world also connected with Pan, Dionysian agents may rule. Surely primal elements are present in the association of caves with preterhuman existence — with rites of birth and death, magic ceremonies, mantic powers, erotic bacchanalian orgies — and in the ubiquity of water.

Elsewhere, I have tried to interpret the Renaissance grotto in terms of ideas embodied in Renaissance Neoplatonism.[8] While concentrating on the usual classical sources, the "darker" side of Neoplatonism accessible to Ficino and the Florentine humanists was stressed. Some light might be shed concerning the influence of those chthonic forces of the Renaissance explored in the works of Agrippa von Nettesheim and Paracelsus on hermeticism. Of particular interest is the role of alchemy noting the correspondence of what is above to that which is below, especially the fundamental principle of alchemy, the law of opposites (as is suggested in the provocative quotation by Rabelais that opens this study).[9]

It is this same world of the occult, the odd Renaissance mixture of pseudo-science with the growing development of the natural sciences, that leads to new forms of the grotto. Thus the magical proponents of the grotto, with its key to the mysteries of nature, are joined to a newly rediscovered technology to create a different species. The element of play in these late Renaissance toys, indicative of a new grasp of the ancient sciences, is based largely on the inventions of the school of Alexandria, the writings of Ctesibius, Philo, and Hero and their survival in the Middle Ages in Arabic texts and Islamic miniatures. The work of Hero ca. the first century B.C. was most influential for the moderns; a Latin translation of *Pneumatica* appeared in the thirteenth century.[10] Problems dealing with the working of siphons, for example, the necessity for air to take the place of water to permit flow, are illustrated, though their solutions awaited the scientific experiments of the seventeenth century. Apparently, the automata designed for the theatre had a powerful effect on late Renaissance gardens and on the works of De Caus.

Leonardo da Vinci, in the citation above (p. vi), gives us a remarkable insight into the ambivalent quality of the grotto. Alternating emotions of repulsion and attraction, of dread and curiosity, are explored in a study on speleolatry, or cave worship, which recognizes that "together with the mountain, or the river, with which it is associated, the cave belongs to a higher order of beings — 'elementals'. . . nature's wonders hidden in strange places."[11]

The magical/mystical properties of caves date from earliest times when caves were the dwelling places of troglodytes who painted their walls to elicit powers of incantation and wonder-working miracles. In the ancient world, the cave is the seat of an oracle, or a place for healing. Virgil describes the cave of the sibyl in the volcanic grotto-hills of Cumae, wherein her piercing response resounded (*Aen*.6.44). Like springs and waters, caves are famous, too, for their particular salutary and curative properties. Pausanius (3.24) tells of a cave "sacred to Asclepius; the image is of stone. There is a fountain of cold water springing from the rock. . . ." Also significant is the magic contact with the rock, the power of self-renewal in the stone.

Beginning in the Mediterranean world, and eventually extending far beyond it, the garden grotto provided a means to create and manipulate the most precious element — water — to regulate and recycle it, to worship and display it. The poetics of water could be attached to the void, to chaos, and to the frozen architecture of stalagmites and stalactites in natural subterranean caverns. Nature always remains the starting point, even when the grotto incorporated the most blatantly unnatural devices, the thousands of shells in such array as to be more suitable for a geological display, or the artful arrangements of stone and moss-covered rocks. But though the ingredients may have been gleaned from nature, their final destiny, as we shall see, was often far removed.

5. *Design for grotesque*, early sixteenth century. Engraving by Master of the Die.

II. METAPHOR OF THE COSMOS: A CLASSICAL TOPOS

> At the head of the harbor, there is an olive tree with spreading leaves, and nearby is a cave that is shaded, and pleasant, and sacred to the nymphs who are called the Nymphs of the Wellsprings,... and there is water forever flowing. It has two entrances, one of them facing the North Wind, where people can enter, but the one toward the South Wind has more divinity. That is the way of the immortals, and no men enter by that way.
>
> Homer, *Odyssey* 13.102-112

The Beginnings: Grotto as Sanctuary

Fragments of sculpture and springs overgrown with vegetation are all that survive of the gardens of ancient Greece, about which we know little indeed. This is due in part to the pattern of Greek political life, that is, to the importance of the *polis* and to a democratic system that did not encourage the development of luxury within the private sector. However, the slim artistic evidence for grottoes, limited largely to representations on vases and reliefs, is countered by the wealth of literary sources. Homer's provocative passage cited above is one of many and served as the inspiration for Porphyry's *De Antro Nympharum*, written in the third century A.D., an exegesis of the Homeric Cave of the Nymphs. Porphyry endowed this grotto with cosmic significance derived from an astrological interpretation of its two entries and from a detailed analysis of Homer's verses.[1] Caves are prominent throughout *The Odyssey*: that of the Cyclops is well known, and equally important is the hollow cave where Calypso harbored Ulysses for seven years, thereby preventing his return to his own land. But this is not all. As Porphyry tells us: "In the most remote periods of antiquity... caves and grottoes were consecrated to gods before temples were ever thought of—the cave of the Curetes to Zeus in Crete, to Selene and Lycean Pan in Arcadia, to Dionysus on Naxos, and everywhere Mithras was known they propitiated this god by means of a cave."[2]

Grottoes were above all sacred places; here homage was given to the divinities of sources and waters. At first this veneration took place in the caves dotting the coast of Greece, such as the immense and dazzling stalagmitic caverns in the Peloponnesus along the bay of Diros. Over time, natural grot-

13

6. Rome, House on the Esquiline. Odyssey frieze, *Arrival in the Land of the Laestrygonians*, late first century B.C. Wall painting. Vatican Museum.

toes were supplanted by artificial ones as the needs of cults expanded and consecrated sanctuaries also served as public utilities for the distribution of water.

An analysis of grottoes in Crete reveals divers roles as sites for pagan cults and as refuges against enemies, whether Dorians, Romans, Arabs, Turks, or Germans (in World War II).[3] Once these caves served as habitats and shelters, fugitive refuges, centers of resistance. Initially used as human dwellings by troglodytes and shepherds, they later became places of burial and divine habitation. The many functions of these sacred caves were matched by the great variety of their forms. We learn of deep grottoes with rooms and galleries carved from rock, such as the caves of Ida and Psycho in Crete and those of Parnassus and Hymetus in Attica; of caves cut into vertical walls, as in the north slope of the Acropolis in Athens; of crevices and natural abysses in the volcanic country of central Greece, the Peloponnesus, or the Cyclades; and of openings along the mountainous coast of the mainland and the islands.

For sheer number of caverns, Crete has no rival—by recent count about 1,400. The ancients looked upon Crete as the place of origin of all the gods (*Diod.*5.64-77); the island is after all the site of the palace of Knossos, the labyrinth of the Minotaur, and the tomb of Zeus. Among the caves mentioned in ancient sources, few have aroused as much interest as the alleged site of the birth of Zeus on Mount Ida. Pythagoras is associated with the cave, where he is believed to have incubated for nine days while in search of enlightenment.[4] Analogies have been noted between certain rituals of Pythagoreanism and those of the Cretan religion as practiced in the cave on Mount Ida.[5]

Although the precise nature of the ancient mysteries and rituals associated with these caves still eludes us, they are epitomized by the fourth-century

14

B.C. Plutonium in Eleusis, the site of Eleusinian mysteries belonging to Demeter. Because of its elevated position above the Sacred Way — with vistas of mountains and sea, this was the course followed by initiates from Athens to Eleusis; it was once lined with tombs, shrines, altars, lustral basins, and fountains — the area containing the cave was immediately open to the view of the initiates as they entered the sacred compound. The procession wound its way to the right of the inner propylaea toward the grotto, once the sanctuary of Pluto, and climbed the steps leading to the temple where the revelations of the mysteries took place. Within the two deep chambers of the sanctuary was a stairway, perhaps used in the staging of Persephone's annual springtime return from the underworld to take part in the celebration of the mysteries, the rites symbolizing nature's cycle of life, death, and rebirth.[6] This idea of the grotto as a place of passage between worlds is reinforced by the imagery of Dionysiac craters, where caves represent sacred passages within which the initiation rites were performed.[7]

The focal position of the hallowed grotto with its inner, secret recesses is apparent even in modern-day Athens. Ascending to the Acropolis from the northwest side, we see the cliffs with grottoes carved into the rock; votive placques are dedicated to Apollo and Pan.[8] Here was the god Pan's principal sanctuary, identified with that cave mentioned by Pausanius (1.28.4): "On descending...to just beneath the Gateway [there is] a fountain and near it is a sanctuary of Apollo in a cave. It is here that Apollo is believed to have met Creüsa, daughter of Erectheus...."[9] This cave was consecrated to Pan following the introduction, with great fanfare, of his cult to Athens, a direct result of his siding with the Athenians in the victory over the Persians in the battle of Marathon. Via a rockhewn stairway, the entry of the grottoes led to the plateau of the Acropolis above.

South of the Acropolis in the Illisson riverbed are the remains of the ancient fountain Callirhoe. Its name, "fair flowing," denotes the spring issuing from the rock, probably the source of Athens' water. This spring has been identified with the nine-spouted Enneakronos erected by the tyrants and used for important ceremonials including those connected with marriage rites.[10]

No cave dedicated to Pan and the nymphs is of more renown than the Corcyrian Cave on Mount Parnassus celebrated for its bacchic orgies. In Aeschylus' *Eumenides* (22-24), the prophetess reveres "the Nymphs, who dwell where is the Corcyrian caverned rock, delight of birds and haunt of powers divine." Pausanius (10.32.2,7) tells us that "the climb to the Korykian [sic] cave is relatively easy for a sturdy man or for mules....From the Korykian cave on it is hard, even for a sturdy man, to attain the peaks of Parnassos...." Recently, the poet George Seferis described his ascent to the Corcyrian Cave, where

> round the cave the nocturnal orgies of the Thyiades and the Maenades used to take place....To the right as you enter the cave you can still see the stone with the half-obliterated inscription to Pan and the Nymphs. Then you have a feeling that you've descended into a vast womb....It's only after you've gone a fair way in and then have turned back that you see like a benediction the parallel rays of the sun entering the cave's mouth....[11]

15

Though ritual founts often lacked visual splendor, they were given monumental character by force of their association with various deities. Celebrated above all sources is the Castalian Fount, the spring sacred to Apollo, which served his temple at Delphi for purification rites. The spring flowed from a rock at the entry of a narrow gorge; here worshippers laved before entering the shrine. Like the Hippocrene, the fountain was also a favorite haunt of Apollo and the Muses and hence considered a source of poetic inspiration.[12] Little exists today to indicate the once magnificent facade hewn from the hard rock and adorned with seven marble pillars crowned by an entablature; the niches once contained statuettes, while seven bronze lions' heads served as conduits for water that flowed down eight steps to a receiving basin. The Greeks praised these waters vital for the worship of Apollo and the function of the oracle. In Euripides' *Ion* (1537-38), the temple of Apollo is sprinkled with this water. Priests submitted to cleansing rites here. Pindaric odes mark the pilgrims' way to the spring, which they visited before consulting the oracle.[13]

The fountains of Corinth, still extant, represent a transitional type that is later incorporated in the grand Roman fountains, or *nymphaea*. Originally open to the sky, sacred fountains here were probably not covered before the fifth century B.C. Dedicated to the daughter of King Creon (in reality a water nymph), the Fountain of Glauke once comprised a porticoed facade behind which was an entry to an artificial grotto: "Into this they say she threw herself

7. Corinth. Fountain of Peirene, second century A.D. (begun third century B.C.).

16

in the belief that the water would be a cure for the drugs of Medea...."
(Pausanius, *Corinth* 2.3.6).

Many legends are attached to the Fountain of Peirene in the Agora of Corinth in use from the earliest times until the end of the nineteenth century. Is this the stream that gushed forth from a stroke of the hoof of Pegasus? The portico itself had undergone major transformations to reach the grand design by Herod Atticus in the second century A.D. Divided into six apses — grottolike chambers — three sides of a quadratic court are grouped about an open-air fountain; the facade was revetted in marble in the third century B.C. Both sacred spring and city reservoir, this splendid monumental fountain encloses the sunken basin with its columnar facade and marble balustrade.[14] What we see today is the second-century A.D. design wherein the fountain is surrounded by an exedra: "The spring is ornamented with white marble, and there have been made chambers like caves, out of which the water flows into an open-air well. It is pleasant to drink. . . ." (Pausanius 2.3.2-3).

Transition: The Nymphaeum

Simple fountain houses in the Athenian Agora were replaced in Roman times by more elaborate hydraulic installations known as *nymphaea*, "fountains consecrated to the nymphs." Religious associations, often of Greek cults relating to sources and to springs, were meant to be evoked by the structures. Of Greek origin, a *nymphaeum* was a temple dedicated to the nymphs. Because these shrines were originally grottoes with springs, the term was later applied both to artificial fountain grottoes and to monumental public fountains from the time of the Roman Empire.[15] In Pliny, the word *nymphaeum* appears alongside thermae and aqueducts, and the purpose of the edifice is often uncertain (*NH*.36.154). This uncertainty has persisted to the present day: is a nymphaeum to be considered a functional hydraulic structure, a means for the display of fountains, an ornamental waterworks system, an auditorium for theatrical presentations, or a museum for the exhibition of sculpture?[16] At Olympia, the monumental exedra of Herod Atticus, built in A.D. 156, reproduces all the aspects of a Roman nymphaeum with its rectilinear basin adorned with statue-filled marble niches. Similar complex fountains were designed in the Hellenistic period as terminals (or reservoirs) for water systems; facades, basins, and porticos were frequently built in front of entries to natural grottoes. Later these were replaced by artificial ones or by apses.[17] Among monumental nymphaea is the early second-century A.D. fountain dedicated to Trajan at Ephesus. It was once a two-tiered structure, thirty-six feet high, where water flowed to the pool beneath the twice life-size statue of the emperor.[18]

Also probably of Hellenistic date, the Grotto of Herakles in Delos is roofed to a peak with inclined slabs of granite in a Cyclopean manner reminiscent of the sybil's cave at Cumae — and more remotely of the Homeric "chamber like caves" at Tiryns. It is an early example of the grotto as gateway, for it was considered a *porte* by ancient travelers and was only recognized as a sanctuary in the eighteenth century.[19]

17

8. Delos. Cave of Herakles, ca. third century B.C. (?).

Descended from classical and eastern Hellenistic prototypes, grottoes became frequent in the late first century B.C. and proliferated during Imperial times when they became commonplace features in the gardens of wealthy patricians. Two principal types are in evidence: the rustic grotto in imitation of a cave and the architectural nymphaeum. A rigorous definition of nymphaeum would limit its designation to sacred edifices that serve as sanctuaries of nymphs, though the term is also applied to Roman pleasure houses with gardens, fountains, and statues.[20] Some scholars restrict the application of the term to monumental fountains, using the word *musaeum*, literally "a temple of the Muses," to designate places sacred to the nymphs. (Note Pliny, *NH*.36.54 who calls the "hollowed rocks in the buildings...museum, an artificial imitation of a cave.") B. Tamm has categorized "*nymphaea* and *musaea* as rooms that are in fact, or resemble, grottoes." She sees them both as types of apse hall, because of the very marked association with grottoes in some halls "with imitation dropstone stalagmites, while others, with their rows of internal columns forming side aisles, remind us of basilicas."[21]

Later, public fountains assume the form of the earlier sanctuaries. In the Roman world one must always distinguish between public and private nymphaea. The former were often independent structures but sometimes were annexed to thermal establishments, palaces, or villas. Occasionally, a public nymphaeum was built on a true source fed by aqueducts that served for the distribution of the waters.[22] One of the most imposing must have been the Nymphaeum Hortorum Licinianorum, whose ruins can be seen today hard by the train tracks of the Stazione Termini in Rome, although it may be more familiar to us in Piranesi's view. The specific purpose of this centrally planned, ten-sided domical structure, more popularly known as the Temple of Minerva Medici, is unknown; very likely it was used ceremonially. Sometimes classified with funerary architecture and centrally planned schemes and thus placed among other mausolea, in the mid-eighteenth century, the middle of the atrium still contained "a fountain with ten semicircles," effectively repeating the perimetal rhythm of the building.[23]

The only extant large public nymphaeum in Rome (and the only one known in the sixteenth century), the Castell dell'Acqua Marcia, or Acqua Julia, is better revealed to us through prints. The lower facade of the monumental fountain dates from the first century A.D., its brick facade from the time of Alexander Severus (A.D. 222-35). Sometimes alluded to as a "triumphal fountain," marble trophies formerly stood in the arched openings, as can be seen in Dupérac's engravings of 1575. These were removed to the Capitol balustrade by Sixtus V in 1590. Serving as a distribution reservoir of water (*castellum aquarum*), it was originally the terminus of the aqueduct built by Agrippa and many times reconstructed. The conduits of today's Julia fountain once led water to different parts of the city.[24] Its grand triumphal arch with statuary and fountains cascading into basins was adopted by the Renaissance popes in their fountains, the Acqua Felice and the Acqua Paola.

Turning to examples of private nymphaea, we note that many more of these survive. As with public nymphaea, the major distinction is between rusticated grottoes in natural caves and nymphaea of an architectural disposition. Among the architectural nymphaea are those with a large niche comparable to the cavea of a theatre and others whose rectangular rooms are terminated by an apse. The apse form was dominant from the second century B.C. to the second century A.D. and exquisitely symbolizes the natural grotto with water gushing from it. It is the cave transformed into art by man, with its double function—religious and utilitarian—intact.[25]

The apse, though decorated as a nymphaeum, constitutes the main feature of the House of the Great Fountain and the House of the Little Fountain in

9. Rome, Acqua Julia (Marcia), first–third centuries A.D. Engraving by A. Sadeler, 1606.

10. Boscoreale, villa near Pompeii. Cubiculum with grotto, first century B.C. Wall painting. New York, Metropolitan Museum of Art.

Pompeii. Fashionable in the post-Augustan era, these fountains were imported from Greco-Roman Egypt.[26] Contrasts abound in the tufa juxtaposed with the graceful and intricate mosaic niche in the background of the great fountain, placed opposite the main entrance. Projecting from the fountain's walls are theatrical masks, while a white marble putto with dolphin adorns the niche. The water in the principal garden repeats on a much reduced scale the sophisticated canalization of the city at large.[27]

Grottoes (and water) frequently form part of the mysterious, numinous, and erotic settings of antiquity, whether in Ovid's poetical landscapes or in pictorial representations.[28] While limited in number, wall paintings provide excellent evidence for the species. Examples range from the rustic shrines in the fresco of the Boscoreale cubiculum with its grotto surmounted by a pergola, ca. 50 B.C., to the Odyssey frieze and the sacro-idyllic landscapes with their rocky groves in Pompeii, Herculaneum, the Palatine, and elsewhere. For example, a painting in Herculaneum shows a young girl seated before a grotto with a row of statuettes of household gods sheltered in the hollow of an enormous rock. This work is interpreted as a "scene" — a satyric drama according to the precepts of Vitruvius.[29]

Such *topoi* were fundamental themes of landscape and used by painters, gardeners, and sculptors to give an impression of nature, albeit an arcadian, quasimythological one.[30] During the time of the late Republic, vistas of grottoes dramatically punctuated the shoreline of the Bay of Naples.[31] Statius (*Silvae* 3.1.144) tells how "the very nymphs of the green waters leap forth unbidden from their pumice caves; they cling to the streaming rocks. . . ." Common in Campania, these caves were often associated with Venus. In this form, the strong connection with the apse was always stressed. Inspired by the shell, the typical and standard decoration became a half dome over an apse, a form particularly appropriate for monuments connected with Venus.

11. Rome. Septizodium, A.D. 203. Engraving by A. Sadeler, 1606.

Grotto as Theatre

Rapports between the nymphaeum and theatrical architecture are fairly well established. Vitruvius (*De Arch.* 5.6.9), for example, uses the grotto as part of the scenery of satyric plays. At the dawn of the Roman empire the illusion of a grotto opening on a garden has become a conventional feature recalling a rustic or theatrical play. And by extension such monumental theatrical structures as the background scene (*frons scaenae*) of Sabratha, the nymphaea of Miletus or Aspendos, the facade of the Library of Celsus at Ephesus, and the Septizodium become identified with one another.

It is therefore probable that the *frons scaenae* in certain theatres was formed by monumental nymphaea. Evidence for the so-called theatre-nymphaea exists in such disparate structures as a nymphaeum at Antioch, the great theatres of the fountains in Pompeii and Ayakto, the Baths of Sosandre at Baiae, and the Villa Pausilypon at Naples. [32] In any event, one must consider the *frons scaenae* and the quadrangular nymphaeum as two versions of an architectural formula often used for other purposes, as for example, the library at Ephesus. Thus, we see that a common mode was employed for different ends — be it actual building, scenic architecture, or the sacro-idyllic repertoire of Pompeian wall painting. It appears too that similar conventions were followed in the painted architecture of the Campanian maritime villas and in the general disposition of such a structure as the Septizodium.

It is Ammianus Marcellinus (15.7.3) who provides an early reference linking the Septizodium and a nymphaeum in describing the people assembled at this "much frequented spot, where the emperor Marcus Aurelius erected a Nymphaeum of pretentious style." Dedicated in A.D. 203 to the seven planets, it was demolished in 1588-89 during Pope Sixtus V's regime, so that its materials could be used in papal buildings. Apparently derived from a North African rather than an Eastern type, the Septizodium has also been discussed in connection with the deep hemicycle of the theatre at Corinth and the one in the fountain of Herod Atticus at Olympia.[33]

21

If the character of the background wall of the three-storied portico at the southeast corner of the Palatine Hill evokes the decor of a theatrical scene, it is perhaps because this decor had already been put into play in the grand nymphaea. This monumental facade replete with fountains was built as an ornamental front to the imperial palace of Septimus Severus on the facade toward the Via Appia, thereby masking the slopes of the Capitoline and forming an impressive backdrop to the Forum (*Hist. Alex. Sever.* 19.5). So would voyagers from Africa glean an idea of the magnificence of the *urbs* and, in particular, the glory of the emperor, whose colossal statue once adorned the central niche. This intention is made clear in the life of Septimus Severus in the *Scriptores Historiae Augustae* (29.3): "When he built the Septizodium he had no other thought than that his building should strike the eyes of those who came to Rome from Africa."

Grotto in the Landscape

Architectural remains allow us to ascertain that in Roman times, the fountain could serve myriad functions. A fountain could be an architectural fantasy about a reservoir of water, a decorative motif in the urban planning of an emperor, a water theatre, or an open air museum. However, its meaning in Roman religion is much more difficult for us to decipher.

Specifically Roman ties to the creation of grottoes are reinforced by the landscapes of Latium and the Campagna Romana to the south of the city. Walls of tufa, the thick crust of old lava and rock—what grottoes are made of in Pliny and Ovid—came into being through volcanic eruptions and formed the ridges around Rome. Eighteenth-century descriptions and maps, such as those by Nolli, give an impression of a series of cryptoportici and nymphaea decorated with pumice and mosaics. But the key to grottoes appears to be in the *forre*, the old watercourses, ravines, and undergrowths in the volcanic crest.[34] The varieties of these interruptions in the Campania, the country surrounding the Gulf of Naples, produce a kind of underworld very different from the surface above. It is a world reminiscent of that inhabited by the wealthy Roman patrician (see Plutarch, *Lucullus*, 39.3) where "on the seashore and in the vicinity of Naples...he suspended hills over vast tunnels...." In Virgil's vast cavern in the underworld, the natural side of the city belongs to the chthonic domain and is described as "beneath a dark rock, the Lupercal, bearing after Arcadian wont the name of Lycaean Pan" (*Aen.* 8.343-45).

Roman vernacular preserved the natural character, the hollowed-out spaces in the tufa rocks. The "arched openings of the *tabernae* still remind us of grottoes excavated in the walls of the *forre*."[35] Perhaps we can best visualize this phenomenon by studying the depiction of Roman ruins, especially works pertaining to the storage and conduction of water, that is, reservoirs, aqueducts, and tunnels. Almost any etching in Piranesi's *Di due Spelonche*...dramatically illustrates the underworld of this region. Here we see two subterranean grottoes which are carved into the cliff that bounds Lake Albano. The one called Ninfeo Bergantino is near the entry of the Emissarium, the tunnel bored through rock in B.C. 396 to regulate the level of the lake; the other is the Ninfeo Dorico, and dates from circa B.C. 50. Ancient inscriptions on the stone record the role of the nymphs, though Piranesi questions the original form and the function of the works. Were they meant for pleasure or bathing? Citing Homer, Virgil, and Martial, Piranesi calls on the poets who described caves as the dwellings of nymphs — caves of natural tufa and of stone, vaulted and with a stone basin receiving water — and further suggests that these caves were probably the site of those Clodian orgies denounced by Cicero.[36]

That grottoes are in some sense a Mediterranean phenomenon is seen by the existence of examples not only in the Roman Campagna and in Tivoli but also in the country around Naples and in the *latomie* of ancient Syracuse. Hewn in the rock, these stone quarries reaching to a depth of from 100 to 103 feet constituted the sources for Syracuse's building materials.[37] Now dense with clinging ivy and wild lavender, the Latomia del Paradiso was once used as a burial place and as a prison for captive enemies who worked in them. Shades of Plato's cave! The grotto carved into the western wall, known as the Ear of Dionysus, is famous for its accoustical properties. Its S-shape parallels that of the adjoining theatre. Nearby, in the Grotta dei Cordari, the rope makers practiced their trade.

Few places testify more vividly to the origin of the grotto than does the Greco-Roman landscape around the Bay of Naples. This coast, lined by the ancient towns of Puteoli, Averna, Baiae, and Misenum, is extremely rich in quarry caves. It has been discovered that the underwater "rocks" in the submerged Greek and Roman foreshore near Naples are artificial in origin, not rocks at all but ancient buildings that have been preserved from weathering by submersion in the deep water, a find corroborated by geological evidence of the fall of the Roman shoreline.[38] One of these was the Greek Pausilypon, or Posilipo, associated with the cave-dwelling Cumaei, who were noted for their sophisticated tunnelings. The Grotto of Posilipo, a marvel of ancient engineering probably built in the time of Augustus (replaced by a new tunnel in the 1880s), 774 yards long, was dark and low; the Grotto of Sejanus as described by Strabo (5.100;4.7) was a tunnel illuminated by shafts of light. Seneca (*Epistulae* 57.1) depicts the trials of travel from Baiae to Naples, the shortcut to Pausilypon, via this tunnel: "No place could be longer than that prison — the torches enabling me to see only darkness; the oppressive duct...the gloom, however, furnished one with some food for thought; I felt a certain mental thrill, and a transformation unaccompanied by fear...."[39]

Of ancient grottoes known to us, scarcely any can rival the marvelous formation of Sperlonga (from the Latin *spelunca*, or cave). Archaeological evidence and learned interpretations have recently reinforced the vivid accounts of Tacitus and Suetonius portraying the collapse of the roof in A.D. 26 when Tiberius was dining there. Sculptures within the grotto form a unified program illustrating Homeric episodes that reveal many facets of Ulysses's character.[40] Boethius describes Sperlonga as a "fantastic cave, with its pools and its four Homeric marble groups and other sculpture, which like a gigantic heathen presepio, faces the sea. . . ."[41] Forming a type of proscenium arch for

23

12. Lake Albano, Castelgondolfo. Ninfeo Bergantino, late first century A.D. Etching by G. B. Piranesi, 1762.

13. Posilipo. View of entrance to grotto. Engraving in P. Panvini, *Il forestiere antichità e curiosità naturali di Pozzuoli*, 1818.

14. Sperlonga. Grotto-triclinium, first century B.C. Engraving by L. Rossini, 1835.

24

the drama within, the grotto is thought to date from the Augustan era. From the outside, one admires the reticulated work, the round and rectangular pools, and the triclinium facing into the cave. The interior was supposedly lined with stucco-bearing frescoed seascapes, and the ground was paved with polychrome marble slabs. Sperlonga is the earliest known to date of a grotto-triclinium, that is, a nymphaeum and a banqueting hall combined, though the aviary of Lucullus in his Campagna villa ca. 59 B.C. (as noted by Varro) may have preceded it. Another worth mentioning is in the House of Loreius Tiburtinus in Pompeii, dating from early Flavian times and provided with rainwater basins. This type is also found in Rome, Stabiae, Sorrento, and elsewhere.[42]

The grotto-nymphaea in the most idiosyncratic of all villas, that of Hadrian, are not easy to analyze. In this vast domain recording the personal history of the emperor's eastern voyages, all is generated by water. Such structures as baths and cryptoportici are related to grottoes, while the grand pools and vaulted temples and island theatres are variants on the basic principle. There are many natural grottoes in the region around Tivoli, and surely it may be said that natural and chthonic forces meet in this strange amalgam of East and West. Several nymphaea at the villa date from Republican times to the fifth century. Cryptoportici throughout form an underground network of *aestivi specus*, shelters from the summer heat, which linked all parts of the villa.[43] While the Maritime Theatre is not a grotto per se, it seems to have served similar purposes. Here was the emperor's favored retreat; here, he pursued his private pleasures and indulged in art, in poetry, and in music.

Hadrian created the Canopus and Serapeum—the canal joining the temple and nymphaeum—in memory of his beloved Antinoos and named it after the Egyptian port near Alexandria sacred to Serapis, one of the incarnations of Osiris. Copies of the Erectheum caryatids and other classical statuary line the long canal leading to the grottolike structure. This canal is adorned with an arched columniated system terminating in the grand apse of the vaulted Temple of Serapis. The Serapeum itself is a vast semicircular hall whose umbrella like half-dome is faced in a white mosaic of alternating spherical and helicoid shapes. A sumptuous monumental nymphaeum—an exedra with the triclinium within—was built against the hill. Richly adorned with marbles, frescoes, and statues of basalt, the Serapeum was above all animated by fountains, jets, and streams of water. An idea of the complex waterworks may be gleaned by a glance at the hydraulic setup placed above and behind the vault.[44] Water descended from a reservoir on top, "issued from the 'grotto' and cascaded down to a pool at the foot of the apse and thence flowed from pool to pool until it eventually reached the euripus (Canopus)."[45] Here Hadrian worshipped Serapis and paid homage to Antinoos who had drowned under mysterious circumstances in the Nile. Both religious and aesthetic associations were thus summoned. Southeast of the Canopus is a long valley cut into the tufa in which there is an artificial grotto known as the Entry to the Underworld. The design of the apse enriched the image, familiar to antiquity, of the rock from which the source flows and that harbors the altar of the

15. Tivoli, Hadrian's Villa. Canopus, view toward Serapium, A.D. 118–138.

16. Rome. Egeria's Nymphaeum, first half of second century A.D. Drawing by F. de Hollanda, 1538–39.

17. Tivoli, Hadrian's Villa. Serapium, A.D. 118–138.

nymphs: "They were near the city, and had come to a well-wrought, fair-flowing fountain, wherefrom the townfolk drew water...and around was a grove of poplars that grew by the waters, circling it on all sides, and down the cold water flowed from the rock above, and on the top was built an altar to the nymphs where all passers-by made offerings...." (*Od.* 17.205-11).

26

Literary Sources

Written sources referring to grottoes and nymphs abound. From accounts of the Mouseion of Alexandria, we know that artificial grottoes were connected with the Muses and with banquets. For example, we read in Livy (1.21.3) that King Numa dedicated the "grove watered by a perennial spring which flowed through the midst of it out of a dark cave" to the Camenae, alleging that they held council there with his wife Egeria." The site of Egeria's council is also portrayed by Juvenal (*Satires* 3.17-22): "We went down to Egeria's Vale and the caves, all artificial now. How much nearer the water-nymph's presence would be felt if green grass bordered the water, instead of marble slabs that insult our native rock!" Juvenal's diatribe is directed against the foreign elements that had invaded Rome; he bemoans the former sylvan groves, like Camenae and the Valley of Egeria, that have lost their ancient associations as the caves "become a travesty of nature."[46] Gazing at the sorry ruin that is the nymphs' domain today, it may be difficult to understand how the once grand nymphaeum of the villa of Herod Atticus could have so appealed to the Renaissance. From the vantage point of the twentieth century, we look to such representations as those by Francesco de Hollanda and Piranesi with a nostalgia that is far indeed from the travesties of nature against which Juvenal rails.

The pastoral, the sacred, the idyllic, the dramatic—all are modes suited to evoking the ancient grotto in its many guises. Remote places for initiates seeking hidden wisdom and inspiration, or scenes of rites and haunts of mantic powers, they are the continual objects of the poets' narrative. There is the cave that is Virgil's underworld: "A deep cave there was, yawning wide and vast, shingly, and sheltered by dark lake and woodland gloom..." (*Aen.* 6.237-38); or the cave inspired by the romantic provocations of Longus and given to dalliance and to love: "The cave they adorned with curious work, set up statues, built an altar of Cupid the Shepherd, and to Pan..." (*Daphnis* 4.39). And, of course, the mysterious and numinous evocations of Ovid: "There is a grotto in this grove, whether made by nature or by art one may not surely say, but rather by art. To this grot oftentimes, riding thy bridled dolphin, Thetis naked wast thou want to come. There then did Peleus seize thee as thou layest wrapped in slumber. . . " (*Met.* 2.234-40).[47]

The tradition that deems the grotto a locus for the seclusion and tranquility sought by the poet is manifest in the imagery of Propertius (3.1.1-6). Like Hesiod and Homer before him, Propertius appealed to the "shades and sacred rites" of Callimachus and Philetas, rites corresponding to the invocations on Mount Helicon: "Tell me, in what grotto did ye spin the fine thread of your song? With what step did ye enter? What sacred fountain did ye drink?" The poet visits the grove (*spelunca*) to consult the oracle; its decorative bric-a-brac suggests the artificial grottoes of the Muses seen at Rome in the villas of the wealthy. He then proceeds to tell of Phoebus in his Castalian grove, which is described as "a green cave, its walls lined with pebbles, and/timbrels hung from its hollowed stones" (3.3.25ff). Here the Muse Calliope, drawing water from the fount, sprinkles the lips of Propertius, urging him to return to write love poetry, thereby affirming the communion of the poet with Apollo and the Muses within the grotto.[48] Suffused with the shades of Dionysus, Pan, and Venus, the grotto of Propertius is, above all, a source of knowledge and inspiration. A century later, Martial goes back to Castalian water as the source of poetic ideas: "Grant me without scathe the delights of thy spring: may my thirst begin without harm" (*Epigrams* 1.6.47).

18. Eleusis, Cave of Persephone, 4th century B.C.

19. Ephesus, Fountain of Trajan, 2nd century A.D.

III. BIBLICAL SOURCES AND CHRISTIAN MYSTERIES

> And men shall enter the caves of the rocks and the holes of the ground, from before the terror of the LORD, and from the glory of his majesty, when he rises to terrify the earth.
>
> *Isaiah* 2.19.

Old Testament: Sanctuaries and Shelters

Caves are preeminent in the Biblical landscape and in the Old Testament. Rarely the sacred haunts of nymphs or the domain of Pan, they are venerated primarily as the resting place of the patriarchs and their progeny. As the grotto was the place where life was generated so, too, life was to come to an end there: "After this, Abraham buried Sarah his wife in the cave of the field of Machpelah east of Mamre (that is, Hebron) in the land of Canaan" (*Gen*.19). Rock-hewn tombs of the Kings and Judges, richly adorned with classical porticoes, may still be seen in Jerusalem's Kidron Valley and attest to these beliefs.

The functions of grottoes in the Holy Land parallel those in the pagan world; here, too, they act as places of passage. In the limestone and sandstone hills, both natural and artificial caves were also sites of early dwellings and served as refuges in times of persecution and oppression. They also were sanctuaries that served as halls of worship. Cisterns for water storage often were within. These reservoirs, hewn of solid rock and lined with masonry, were a common feature in a land with few springs. Archaeological excavations around Mount Carmel, Jerusalem and the Judaean hills, and near the Dead Sea have confirmed Biblical texts reporting the presence of cisterns in caves.[1]

As in the ancient world, grottoes also could be places of revelation. For example, Elijah heard the voice of the Lord after his flight through the desert (I *Kings* 19:9) in a cave on Mount Horeb. On Mounts Carmel and Tabor, twelfth-century hermits founded the Carmelite order; here, grottoes were transformed into subterranean churches. Seventeenth-century representations by pilgrims to Mount Carmel depict a landscape literally dotted with caves and founts dedicated to Elijah and the prophets and peopled by hermits and monks.[2] The sanctity of caves is, thus, linked with hermit-saints and ascetics, as in the rock-cut monastic caves in Cappadocia or the Cave of the Seven Sleepers in Ephesus, which is tied to the hideaway of Christian martyrs who miraculously awoke after a 200-year sleep to confirm the emperor's faith in the resurrection.

Legend vies with archaeological and historical fact in the history of the grottoes of the Holy Land. Among the largest caves are those known as King Solomon's quarries, or in ancient days as Zedekiah's grotto, which are just northeast of the Damascus Gate in the Old City of Jerusalem. Dubbed the Gate of the Grotto in the early Middle Ages, they may be identified with Josephus' "sepulchral caverns of the Kings" (*The Jewish War* 5.42). Part of these subterranean quarries, whose rugged stone roofs were supported by huge pillars, was used as a storehouse for wool in the fifteenth century. Today, masonic symbols carved on the interior survive to indicate the secret meeting places of freemasons, who wielded their instruments of peace in the time of Solomon, when the cave's stone was quarried for the Holy Temple. Folklore dominates the history of today's Moslem sanctuary standing opposite, once the so-called grotto of Jeremiah, whose cistern is lighted from above.[3] Within the Court of the Prison, Jeremiah is said to have composed his Lamentations (*Jer.*38:7-14).

Pagan Themes: Conversions

Yet pagan gods, too, survive in the Holy Land. We can turn to the grotto in ancient Caesaria of Philipi, at the source of the Jordan, which was once the sanctuary of Pan. Josephus, with characteristic hyperbole, describes Paneas (today called Banias) as the site of a cave that lay beneath Herod's temple: "A dark cave opens itself; within which there is a horrible precipice, that descends abruptly to a vast depth; it contains a mighty quantity of water, which is immoveable. . . " (*The Jewish War* 21.933-34). This grotto is set against the snow-clad peaks of Mount Hermon in a town with all the accoutrements of a Greco-Roman village and was a strategic site of pagan worship. Here, Pan and the nymphs and satyrs were venerated. The inhabitants of the country still call it "cavern of the beginning of the source."[4]

"You who pursue deliverances, you who seek the Lord; look to the rock from which you were hewn, and to the quarry from which you were digged" (Isaiah 51:1). As in the Aegean cultures, the cave in Biblical times could be considered as an abbreviation of the cosmos — its vault the sky, its ground the earth. The matrix of the world and of man, it is associated with seasonal rituals; within, the sun, the moon, and the stars are born.[5] Tied to the seasons and to the movements of the sun and the planets, the grotto is on the edge of chaos; it is the primordial substance. The magic contact with the rock is present in both pagan and Christian mysteries, as well as in those of Mithraism, an oriental cult propagated in Rome in the first century A.D. Compare Mithras's legendary birth from the supposedly divine rock, his association with the sun and other heavenly bodies, his adoration by shepherds, the subsequent ritual of the capture and sacrifice of the bull, and the rites of initiation, which include a kind of baptism, with events in the life of Christ. All

30

20. *Mithras Sacrificing the Bull,* mid-sixteenth century. Engraving by P. Ligorio.

of these Mithraic rites took place in natural or artificial grottoes. A late sixteenth-century engraving of Mithras sacrificing the bull shows an altar still in situ in the subterranean Mithraeum below the Ara Coeli.[6]

Attempts have been made to link the Christian grottoes with their pagan antecedents, that is, the ceremonies of one may be connected to the existence of the others. Oriental texts and the writings of the church fathers are given as evidence.[7] For example, the grotto where Jesus was born is identified with that of Adonis in its Syrian and Dionysian form (St. Jerome's text, Ep.58; *Ad Paulinum;* P.L.28.58). Among the analogies that have been postulated between the events in the life of Christ and that of Adonis (or Attis, the Syro-Phonecian god) is that of the resurrection. The connection of the grotto of Olives, the holy place of supreme revelations, has been made with the passage in Porphyry (32) commenting on the significance of the olive tree, the plant of Athena, near the Homeric cave: "The olive tree planted near the cave, the image of the Cosmos, is a symbol of the wisdom of God." Not by chance is the cave near the olive, a symbol of divine wisdom.[8]

Christian Sacred Sites: Symbolic Allusions

By far the strongest parallels with the grottoes of antiquity are the grottoes that were the site of crucial events in the life of Jesus and those associated with the Virgin.[9] Before Constantine, Christian churches were unobtrusive; hence, the preponderance of natural caves serving as oratories to shelter the faithful against the elements and providing appropriate places for devotion and the revelation of mysteries.[10] These Christian mysteries occurred in grottoes that are akin in form and in function to the subterranean sanctuaries of the pagans. For example, the mystery of the Annunciation took place in the Grotto of Nazareth, not far from the well where Mary drew water. The foun-

21. *Adoration of the Magi*, ca. 1450. Painting by G. di Paolo. Washington, D.C., National Gallery of Art.

tain of the Virgin was deemed a source of life. Bethlehem is the locus of the Grotto of the Nativity where the "Divine Savior took on human flesh." Nearby is the Milk Grotto, where the Holy Family may have found shelter on the flight into Egypt; named for Mary's milk, which was said to have dropped on the ground and created the chalky rock, it became a place of pilgrimage for nursing women. Like Jesus, John the Baptist was born in a grotto commemorated today beneath the Franciscan church of St. John in Ein Kerem.

Eusebius in his *Life of Constantine* tells how the holy places became "conspicuous and worthy" and pilgrims came to the Holy Land from afar. The mysteries at the heart of the faith were proclaimed in new and glittering buildings in the three holy caves at Bethlehem, Golgotha, and the Mount of Olives.[11] Nowhere are the accretions of history more dense, and hardly is a site more sacred, than is the Mount of Olives, a ridge rising from the ravine of the Kidron Valley, the valley of the tombs in the east of Jerusalem. At the foot of the mount is the Garden of Gethsemane. Here is the sepulchre of the Virgin and a holy well allegedly fed by a source with magic and creative powers. Nearby is the *Antrum Agoniae*, the site of the Agony where Jesus withdrew with his disciples on the evening preceding the Passion. This cave was probably a true grotto carved in the solid rock; the hole pierced in the ceiling permits light to enter and further indicates its earlier function as a cistern or oil press (logical, indeed, in a landscape once marked by the abundance of olive groves).[12] Toward the summit of the mount is the so-called Grotto of the Ascension: the mystic grotto where Christ left the world. It is in this grotto that Jesus "prayed with His disciples and handed on to them the mysteries of perfection" (Eusebius, *Hist. Eccl.* 3.44).[13] It is thus opposed to that of Bethlehem, where Christ came into the world.

32

22. Jerusalem, Dome of the Rock. Cave beneath foundation stone. Engraving by C. Wilson, *Picturesque Palestine*, 1880.

Within the Basilica of the Holy Sepulchre is the Grotto of Calvary (or Golgotha): "the divine grotto. . .buried under a mass of packed earth. . . ." Constantine "embellished the sacred Grotto, the divine monument as the principal part of the whole. . . . The Emperor's magnificence in decorating this centerpiece with selected columns of abundant ornamentation. . .made the venerable grotto shine under a glittering adornment" (Eusebius, *Life of Constantine*, 3:26, 33, 34, 36). Like the sepulchre, the rock-hewn tomb in which Jesus was laid (according to the Gospels, the church fathers, and recent archaeological evidence) was once outside the city's walls.[14]

Fascination with the grotto is rooted in the story of creation. While understood as a source of life and as a sacred spring in the classical world, in the Old Testament the grotto is often equated with the void and hence with chaos — the formlessness that precedes the beginning. As related in Genesis, it was out of this void that the firmament was born and all vegetation and the flying birds and creeping things and beasts of the earth. For example, within the Temple in Jerusalem, beneath the Stone of Foundation in the Dome of the Rock, was a cave known as the Well of Souls.[15] This fountain of perennial water within the Temple preserve may well allude to the cisterns and reservoirs known to be under the Holy Rock, but it also has metaphysical significance and refers to the mouth of the abyss identified with the subterranean torrent located at the earth's center, from whence the rivers of Paradise went forth to water the four corners of the world, a theme that was revived in the paradisal gardens of the Renaissance.

If we are seeking visual parallels to Christian mysteries — in a didactic or mimetic rather than in a spiritual sense — we do well to refer to later eras. Long before grottoes became standard props in the princely gardens of the humanist world, they appeared in the depictions of Christian narratives and early became conventionalized. For example, the Cave of the Nativity and the Sepulchre of the Entombment figure prominently in Byzantine frescoes and mosaics and in late Medieval and Renaissance paintings. Among the most well-known examples are Leonardo's *Madonna of the Rocks* which has been beautifully explored by Chastel for all its grottolike qualities as well as for its mystery, and the countless versions of the *Adoration of the Magi* as painted by Mantegna and Giovanni di Paolo among numerous others.[16] Caves are prominent features in the landscapes forming the backgrounds of paintings of the lives of saints and in the rockscapes of northern miniatures by artists whose patrons had themselves often undertaken the pilgrimage to the Holy Land.

IV. Humanist Conceits: Renaissance Gardens

> The ancients used to dress the Walls of their
> Grottoes and Caverns with all Manner of rough
> Work, with little Chips of Pumice. . . ; and
> some I have known dawb them over with green
> Wax, in Imitation of the mossy Slime which we
> always see in moist Grottoes. I was extremely
> pleased with an artificial Grotto which I have
> seen of this Sort, with a clear Spring of Water
> falling from it; the Walls were composed of
> various Sorts of Sea-shells, lying roughly
> together, some reversed, some with their
> Mouths outwards, their Colours being so artful-
> ly blended as to form a very beautiful Variety.
>
> Alberti, *Ten Books on Architecture*, 9.4[1]

Revival of Classical Prototypes

By the time of the Renaissance, most classical villas were in shambles and their gardens and grottoes wereunrecognizable. But if fifteenth-century archaeological explorations could provide little concrete evidence of antique gardens, the humanists were cognizant of them through extant ancient writings. The poets described this landscape of ruins with eloquence. Boccaccio wrote of Lake Averno and Jacopo Sannazaro of the Cave of the Sybil while in his villa near Virgil's tomb. As in antiquity, philosophical discourses were held in cavelike settings within enclosed gardens.[2] The humanists, men of letters, became advisors to the popes and princes determined to resurrect the ancient world. Building their suburban villas and grounds on presumed Roman models, these enlightened patrons were likely to include one of the garden's principal accessories—the grotto.

Renaissance grottoes, like those of antiquity, may be classified according to architectonic and rustic modes. Despite the extraordinary differences between the architectural nymphaeum and the rustic grotto, both were born of the same spirit and served the same purpose.[3] Often an architectural facade hides the world of simulated nature within. Ambiguity was the key, and the disparity we frequently encounter between the exterior and the interior in the mid- to late sixteenth-century grottoes is surely part of the dominant contemporary aesthetic of mannerism. The beginnings of the style may be traced to Francesco Colonna's romance, the *Hypnerotomachia Poliphili*, first published in Venice in 1499. The "Dream-love-strife of Poliphilus" is a nostalgic reverie of antiquity,

23. Nymphaeum, interior. In F. Colonna, *Hypnerotomachia Poliphili*, Venice,
1499. Woodcut attributed to J. Goujon
(ed. Paris, 1546).

24. Florence, Boboli Gardens.
Grotticello. Fountain of Venus,
Giambologna, 1573.

replete with nymphs and nymphaeum, and putti, and even the mechanical
contrivances that would become hallmarks of the grotto by the mid-sixteenth
century.

Alberti's oft cited passage opening this chapter proves his familiarity with the
ancient practices of designing grottoes as recounted in Pliny and in Ovid. The
former tells us: "We must not forget to discuss also the characteristics of
pumice. This name, of course, is given to the hollowed rocks in the buildings
called by the Greeks 'Home of the Muses,' where such rocks hang from the ceiling so as to create an artificial imitation of a cave" (*NH*.36.154). And in Ovid's
Metamorphosis (3.157-62), we read: "There was a vale in that region . . . the
sacred haunt of high-girt Diana. In its most secret nook there was a well-shaded
grotto wrought by no artist's hand. But Nature by her own cunning had im-
itated art; for she had shaped a native arch of the living rock and soft tufa." Little is known of the grottoes of Alberti's day, with such exceptions as those
recorded as in the D'Este gardens in Ferrara in the 1470s. However, the artificial grotto he describes has analogies with that paragon of artificial grottoes,
the Grotta Grande, which was completed by Duke Francesco I de' Medici in
the Boboli Gardens in Florence in 1593.[4] Here is surely an example of a
Renaissance grotto with classical prototypes, its walls covered with chalky
limestone and adorned with figures in scenes of painted stucco. The work of
man is thus camouflaged by a panoply of natural matter—stalactites,
stalagmites, and all manner of moss-grown rock. At the same time, the grotto
setting acts as a showpiece for works of art. Begun in 1583 according to the
plans of Bernardo Buontalenti, the lower part of the facade was designed by
Vasari in 1556-60 as the terminal point of the corridor that provided a connection between the Uffizi Gallery and the gardens of the Pitti Palace. The
elaborately adorned facade with Baccio Bandinelli's figures of Apollo and Ceres
in niches is opposite the garden entry. Crowned by the Medici arms, the whole
is a marvelous specimen of scenography reminiscent of Vasari's Uffizi facade.

25. Florence, Boboli Gardens. Grotto facade, lower story by G. Vasari, 1556–1560; expansion by B. Buontalenti, 1583–1593. Pen and ink and watercolor by unknown artist (England?), ca. 1790. New York, Cooper-Hewitt Museum.

It is also the first of a series of nymphaeum-facades that hark back to such examples as the facade of the House of Neptune and Amphitrite in Herculaneum.[5]

Duke Cosimo's acquisition of the four unfinished slaves by Michelangelo, originally intended for Julius II's tomb, served as the immediate impetus for the completion of the grotto and its supporting vaults. Indeed, the *non-finito* of these statues is in harmony with the rough-hewn qualities of the grotto, the white marble prisoners standing apart but somehow interwoven with the spongelike surface, the stalactite surroundings, the odd creatures, and the accoutrements of art and nature, the whole forming a strange tableau. Michelangelo's beings, bursting from their natural bounds, are in direct antithesis to the more classical inhabitants of the grotto. Contrarieties abound in this domain where water once streamed from pipes concealed in the *rocaille* and daylight filtered into the grotto through the central vaulted oculus of the cupola, which had been transformed into an aquarium.[6]

What an extraordinary summer retreat for the meditation of the wonders — and secrets — of nature is the Grotta Grande, especially if we imagine the chambers with Vincenzo de' Rossi's *Theseus and Helena* in the mid-space and beyond, in the third grotto chamber, Giambologna's *Venus* rising from a bath on whose rim four satyrs are perched. Visible from the exterior, Bernardino Poccetti's frescoes of fantastic Alpine landscapes celebrate the perfection of art in a natural surrounding; curious figures of shepherds and their flocks, formed from the calcerous aggregate, are on one wall, with nymphs and river gods opposite. The overwhelming impression is that of a ruin resurrected; it is the *idea* of antiquity incarnate. The cupola opening to the sky rises from the vaulted trompe l'oeil fragments; the overgrown moss and plants within, the peeling painted frescoes, the porous excrescences simulating decay and desolation — all mask the architectural framework and are masked in turn. Buontalenti's desire to combine living plants with stone architecture is apparent in a

37

26. Castello, villa near Florence. Grotto, before 1550, N. Tribolo.

watercolor, circa 1790, showing the pedimental gable crowned by agaves rising from hidden terra-cotta pots.[7]

Just a few miles outside Florence is the villa of Castello, once the country seat of Cosimo I de' Medici. Here, in these sixteenth-century gardens, we have one of the earliest coherent garden programs to celebrate the glory of the Medici and of Florence and Tuscany, an allegory devised by Duke Cosimo and his sculptor Tribolo, in collaboration with the writer Benedetto Varchi. Through their efforts, the garden is united in theme as well as in form with the villa. The deep grotto is part of the axial scheme that connects the villa to the sloping terrain and is situated within the garden's enclosing wall. The exterior portal does not betray the fantastic world within. We leave behind the heat of day upon entering this grotto, always cool by virtue of perpetually flowing streams. Within is a veritable menagerie: assorted aquatic vertebrates and crustacea, elephants, buffaloes, and a unicorn who occupies the central position, and myriad shells and coral. Some of the shells and coral are deployed to form masks, while others are combined with tufa and arranged in geometric patterns to form the arched vaults. "All sorts of animals, copied to the life, spouting out by the water of these fountains, some by the beak, others by the wing, some by the nail or the ears, or the nostrils. . . "—so wrote Montaigne of this delightful place in 1580.[8]

This is the grotto that Vasari chose to describe in his introduction when he discussed rustic fountains made with stalactites and incrustations from water such as those used by Duke Cosimo at Castello.[9] In his "Life of Tribolo," Vasari gives a more precise account of the grotto, with its water conduits and its allegorical sculptural representations of the River Mugnone rising in Monte Asinaio and the city of Fiesole emerging from the porous rock and bearing the device of the city.[10] The theme of the earthly paradise is linked to the palace and to the garden as a whole, and the city of Florence and its surroundings are glorified through personifications of the Arno and Mugnone, seen as sources of the fertility of the city and symbols of the greatness of the house of the Medici. The water purified by the unicorn's horn "streams through the lands of the Medici to the figure of Florence, in the allegorical sense an allusion to the existence of the Florentines, now freed from all needs and barbarism, for whom the rule of the Medici has brought a new Golden Age."[11] The humanists in the Medici court, familiar with Virgil's pastoral *Fourth Eclogue*, would readily understand this allusion to a Golden Age: "Earth will pour forth her bounty, animals will live in harmony with one another, and men will not feel the strain of toil" (18-46; 37ff). And like the fountains which act as the backdrops for the sequences in the *Hypnerotomachia Poliphili*, the grotto provides the locus for the telling of the ancient narrative.

A somewhat reduced version of the Castello grotto can be seen at one end of the Room of Hercules, which served as the dining hall of the Farnese Palace at Caprarola begun in 1559. A deep niche includes a marble water basin surrounded by putti and a sleeping cupid. Above is a topographical view of Rome that focuses on the Tiber. The setting of this particular work is in keeping with the classical concepts determining the program as a whole, in particular those aspects relating to the use of grottoes as dining rooms.[12] Outside on the hillside above the palace, the plaza of the small casino is defined by two rusticated stone grottoes below, between which a water stair, or *catena d'acqua*, flows down the center of the ramp; these two grottoes are seventeenth-century additions by Rainaldi. A stepped incline leads to another plaza where two gigantic river gods recline above a rusticated grotto.

This grotto-type, in which the outside contrasts with the inside and in which the artifice is camouflaged and incorporated into the materials of nature while the facade is dominated by an architectonic system, coexists with another form of Renaissance grotto, one that is a more direct imitation of the grand imperial nymphaeum, such as the architectural exedra based on Hellenistic fountain types in the villas of Domitian or Hadrian. In this sphere, the classical nymphaeum par excellence is that of the Villa Giulia. Pope Julius III restored the ancient Acqua Virgo and had its waters led to his villa. The penchant for classicism of the pope and his architects—Vasari in charge together with Ammanati and Vignola, with Michelangelo as advisor—is apparent in the villa's function as an immense antiquarian museum, inspired by the Belvedere and the palaces and villas of the cardinals in Rome. The inscription on the medal coined in 1552 to commemorate the completion of the villa, FONS VIRGINIS VILLAE JULIAE (Fountain to the Virgin of the Villa Giulia), stresses the significance of the nymphaeum as part of the total complex. Images derived from classical texts on Roman waterworks were used by humanists and architects alike to speak of the pope's nymphaeum, reinforcing its links to the ancient Acqua Virgo; for example, Claudio Tolomei's letter dated July 26, 1543 discourses on the aqueducts of Rome and on the new mode of making fountains and speaks of "that beautiful water, which was so clear and so pure, that truly it appeared *vergine* as it was called."[13]

Richly embellished, the nymphaeum of the Villa Giulia at the terminus of the central axis of the palace is the climax of the entire plan. Through the entry we pass into a semicircular courtyard before reaching Ammanati's loggia facing the villa's garden side from which point one may look down on the nymphaeum. Situated on a lower level, the formal hemicycle is now marked by an elliptical staircase. Secret passages in the side walls lead to the *Fontana Segreta* of the Acqua Vergine, the lower water grotto described by Ammanati as the "ultimate in beauty of the entire building, whether by (dint of) the quantity of marbles and ancient and mixed statues or whether by (dint of) the most beautiful Acqua Vergine."[14] Within the grotto at the rear of the nymphaeum on the level above are located on either side hidden spiral stairs giving access to the upper loggia and private garden beyond.[15] Here, within the cavernous chambers with water dripping through the moss-covered rocks, was true respite from the heat of summer and a rustic contrast to the classically ordered system above. Four caryatids guard the entry to the grotto, while its vault is adorned with stucco reliefs illustrating the history of the aqueduct as recounted by Frontinus.[16] In Frontinus's treatise Julius III could find a rationale for the public aspect of the Roman water supply. Falda's engraving reveals other features of this nymphaeum celebrating the pope and his restoration of the old Acqua Virgo. The *frons scaenae,* the eastern facade, is adorned with antique statues of Hercules, Pan, and Bacchus along with Ammanati's reclining river

27. Caprarola, Farnese Palace. Room of Hercules with rustic grotto, 1559–1573.

gods, representing the rivers Tiber and Arno, and what appears to be a majestic prophet in the central niche. Triton-bearing putti on sea-horses are perched on the balustrade, while urn-bearing satyrs dispense the precious element into the granite basin.

The villa was highly praised in its time.[17] Palladio, a visitor to Rome in 1554, was struck by the newly completed work—its stuccos, its fountains, even the way in which semicircles are represented throughout its plan.[18] All this would later be reflected in the nymphaeum of the villa at Maser that he designed for Daniele Barbaro in 1558. Here he joined the nymphaeum cut into the hillside to the villa, the whole breathing the air of a classical Roman enclosure. Statues within niches of the hemicycle were in accord with a program laid out by the Barbaro brothers. Stuccoed, painted, and profusely decorated, the fountain forms a backdrop to the fish pond, from whence water flows to irrigate the gardens.[19]

The proliferation of grottoes in the Renaissance—more specifically in Rome in the early sixteenth century—is part of the revival of classical villas and gardens. As in most Renaissance matters, Petrarch leads the way; he summarizes the grotto as an essential feature of the life of *otium* (leisure), when he praises his Vaucluse retreat with its grotto at the source of the Sorges.[20] From here he writes to Francesco Nelli in the summer of 1352, only regretting that such a garden is not in Italy: "Nearby. . .is seen as suspended a vaulted curve [cave] of living rock which with serene sky defends me from the summer heat. No place could be more inviting to study; and similar to that, but not embellished by the nearby flow of the Sorges, was by chance the small grotto where it pleased Cicero to declaim."[21]

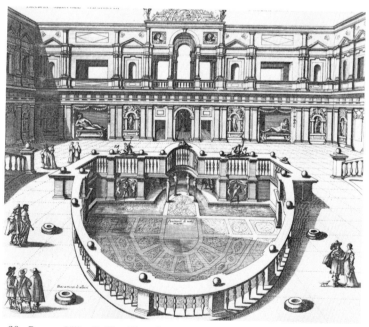

28. Rome, Villa Guilia. Nymphaeum, 1550–1555, B. Ammanati. Engraving after H. Cock in G. B. Falda, *Le fontane di Roma*, ed. 1675–91 (?).

29. Genazzano. Nymphaeum, ca. 1508-1511, attributed to D. Bramante.

"*At secura quies et nescia fallere vitae.* Yet theirs is a repose without care, and a life that knows no fraud (but is rich in treasures manifold)." These words from Virgil's *Georgics* (2.467) are chiseled below the statue of a shepherd in repose, above the entry to the grotto of the garden of Cardinal Rodolfo Pia da Carpi. On the northern edge of the Quirinal Hill, this garden was inspired by that of the humanist Colucci. Here, however, the sleeping nymph is given the setting of a rocky grove. A poem celebrating the presence of the nymph was composed by Marcantonio Flamini in 1547.[22]

Astonishing both as a nymphaeum and as an ambient for leisure is that archaeological resurrection known as the Casino of Pius IV, which is in the gardens of the Vatican. The casino and the loggia designed for the pope by Pirro Ligorio are the ideal retreat. Here is a panoply of antiquity—aquatic and pastoral motifs combine to herald the Golden Age to be brought about by Pius IV's election to the papacy on December 25, 1559. The interior program reiterates doctrines proclaimed by the Council of Trent, specifically "Baptism or the salvation and admission to the Church by the sacrament of water and the Primacy of the Pope."[23] Thus in a sense, the interior assumes the classical aspect of the ancient fountain house or nympaeum with its emphasis on the sacredness of water and on the rites attendant to purification and blessing. Devotion to the nymphs undergoes here a Christian conversion; the memory of the gods of antiquity survives only on the exterior. These pagan beings are barred from the inner sanctum.

Throughout the Renaissance, the grotto remains a domain of contemplation, a world of illusion within a country-seat. As a place of repose for the prince, it could be designed to express the source of his munificence and thereby the renewed power of man, the church, and God. Echoing the transition from the relatively modest villas of Republican Rome to the resplendant ones of the Empire, the quiet retreats of the fifteenth-century papal princes become the luxurious palaces of the sixteenth century. For example, the once secluded court of the Belvedere of Innocent VIII was transformed under Julius II into the grandest of all classical villas, whose plan owes much to the great imperial villas in Rome and in Tivoli.[24] The villa garden, theatre, and statue court in the Belvedere were meant for the cultivation and enjoyment of antiquity. One of the ancient marbles in the statue court was the reclining nymph Ariadne, which was installed as part of a fountain in 1512 and represents the beginning of a form not uncommon in humanist courts.[25] Reminiscent of the ancient Grotto of Egeria, this type is clearly illustrated in Francesco de Hollanda's drawings (1538-39) of such ancient statues as the river gods in their prominent rustic settings, which date from the period of the completion of the court during the pontificate of Paul III (1534-50).[26]

As Alberti is the spokesman for the new style, so Bramante is the architect who best exemplifies its form. Magnificient in its ruins, reminding one of the frigidarium of ancient thermae, and constructed on a scale consonant with the then rising core of St. Peter's, is the nymphaeum, or summer pavilion built for Cardinal Pompeo Colonna outside the town of Genazzano near Palestrina. This nymphaeum, replete with its own artificial lake, is attributed to Bramante and dated circa 1508-11.[27] The remains of a dam nearby suggest the possibility that it was also the setting for water spectacles recalling ancient *naumachiae* (mock naval battles).[28] The facade is almost a theatrical *frons scaenae*—a backdrop for the waterworks, which could be viewed from the opposite slopes or valley.

Accent on the Grotesque

Antonio da Sangallo planned the Villa Madama for Cardinal Giulio de' Medici, who later became Pope Clement VII. Vasari attributes the villa's nymphaeum, dated 1519-23, to Giovanni da Udine. Set into a cleft in Monte Mario at the northwest end of a hippodrome, it is built "in the rustic manner, . . . Its site in the bed of a stream overhung with shrubs and plants. . .caused water to fall through tufa and other stones in drops and slender streams, which had all the appearance of being entirely natural. In the uppermost part of this grotto or cavern, and amidst spungeous stones which formed it he placed a colossal head of a Lion. . .inconceivably charming."[29] It was Giovanni da Udine together with Giulio Romano and Baldassare Peruzzi who painted the loggia *alla grottesca*, that is, in imitation of the underground grottoes rediscovered in the Renaissance.

No structure more effectively illustrates the mockery of architecture — almost its very negation — than does the garden grotto. As John Shear-man has written, it is this essential duality between art and nature that makes the grotto such a perfect specimen of mannerism. Is it "a cave cut in architectural form out of the rock, or, alternatively, architecture overlaid with the dense accretions of time?"[30] The rustic mode, disseminated by Giulio Romano and the followers of Raphael in the Palazzo del Te, was further propagated in the writings of Serlio and was particularly suitable to the idea of the grotto in its advocation of the imitation of natural stone and moss-covered tufa. Nowhere is this art/nature dichotomy better expressed than in Tolomei's letter cited above: "The *ingegnoso artifizio* newly rediscovered of making fountains, which indeed is seen in use in more places in Rome, where mingling art with nature, one cannot discern if it was the work of the former or the latter; thus some appear as natural artifice, and others as artful nature: in such a way they contrive in these times to assemble a fountain, that seems to be made by nature herself, not by chance, but with masterly artistry" (see footnote 13).

Among the earlier rusticated grottoes is that of the Palazzo del Te in Mantua known to us largely via the description of Jacopo Strada. Part of a complex of four chambers, this particular grotto also included a loggia and courtyard "near the secret garden" (the private garden reserved for Federico II Gonzaga) designed circa 1531-32. Documents show that "great expenses" for shells used in its design were incurred as early as 1528. Thus Giulio Romano can be said to have revived the ancient Roman custom of decorating fountains, niches, and baths with shell-encrusted work. Partly created by Giovanni da Udine in the Villa Madama, the mode spread to France (where it later became known as *rocaille*). We may hypothesize that the Te grotto — like the palace room — depicted aspects of the life of Duke Federico II Gonzaga and celebrated his virtues.[31]

Even more crucial for the design of the Te grotto was the grotto of Isabella d'Este in the nearby Palazzo Ducale, which was completed circa 1508. Adjacent to Isabella's studiolo, the small anticamera of the grotto served as a museum providing a combination of *studium* and *otium*; an adjoining corridor led to the enclosed "secret garden." The studiolo was adorned with allegorical paintings depicting Minerva expelling the Vices; its Ovidian motto "otia si tollas/ periere/ cupidinis arcus," recommended study as a remedy for vice.[32] Isabella's only criterion for Giovanni Bellini and the Venetian engraver, Franceso Anichino — "He is free to follow his own fantasy provided that he selects something antique" — may be applicable to the entire grotto. In its massing of curiosities and precious stones and in its cramped quality, the grotto recalls the later *Wunderkammer*. In common with its classical prototypes, it contained a collection of statuary and was a showpiece for visitors to Mantua and a meeting place for humanists.

Architecture of Water

Nowhere is water more truly the queen of all elements than at the Villa d'Este in Tivoli. Sounds of water music in the garden drown out the babble of tourists'

30. Tivoli, Villa d'Este. *Diana of Ephesus*, ca. 1565–1572.

31. Tivoli, Villa d'Este. Oval fountain, the Grotto, ca. 1565–1572, P. Ligorio. Engraving by J. Furtenbach, *Architectura recreationis*, Augsburg, 1640.

voices. Here the purpose of the grotto is as evident as it once was in the nearby Villa of Hadrian — it is to be a cooling reservoir and a source of springs. The dynamic aspect of the water and its sonic range is paralleled and underscored by our movement toward and away from this theatre of infinite aquatic plays. Trees and verdure are laid out in such a manner as to conceal the fountains and grottoes, which spark our wonder and surprise as they are revealed at every turn.

The Villa d'Este, like Hadrian's Villa, provides a feast of nymphaea. Here there are waterworks of every manner, shape, and contrivance, some in architectural frames as elaborate as that of the great hydraulic organ set on the principal cross axis, its ornate frontispiece embellished with four herms and the Este eagle at its summit. The focus of the villa was once the travertine statue of Diane of Ephesus (Nature, or Fortuna, is now placed along the lower perimetal wall) behind which was concealed the organ. Invented in 1568 by the French fountain expert Lucha Clerico, water power propelled the organ to produce music. The powerful jets and the cascade (seventeenth-century additions by Bernini) beyond the three fish ponds rose against the water-organ facade; through falling waters one might have glimpsed the incompleted colossal Neptune at the far end of the axis. Behind the organ just below the uppermost level is a series of three grottoes, very cool and very wet, the water spreading to form gigantic fans and a dazzling vertical veil. The sound is loud but the key contrapuntal to the great organ. On the second cross-axis is the Fountain of Dragons, the Avenue of One-Hundred Fountains, and the Fountain of Rome, which is built on a semicircular terrace with Rome triumphant. Because the theme of the garden was the choice of Hercules, the perpendicular axis was made dominant, forcing spectators to decide which road to take. Montaigne, among others, was dazzled by "that gushing of endless jets of water, held in check and released by a single spring which may be touched a long way off. . . . The music of the organ is effected by means of water which falls with great force into a round arched cave. . . ."[33]

45

32. Tivoli, Villa d'Este. Rustic fountain, *Sleeping Venus*. Interior, ca. 1565–1572. Engraving by G. F. Venturini, *Le fontane di Roma*, Rome, 1675–91 (?).

33. *Design for a Fountain with Pegasus*, second half sixteenth century. Pen and ink and wash drawing by J. Zucchi. Paris, Louvre.

This glorious retreat erected for Ippolito II d'Este, Cardinal of Ferrara, was begun in 1550 following his defeat for the papacy in favor of Julius III. Great expansion of the Tivoli Gardens occured in the 1560s with the arrival of French fountaineers and the archaeologist and collector of ancient Roman statues Pirro Ligorio. Among the more extraordinary nymph/grotto fountains built at this time was the Oval Fountain (the Ovato), or the Fountain of Tivoli, "the principal one of all the fountains of the garden and perhaps of all Italy," according to a Parisian description of the gardens written about 1571.[34] A semicircular basin is engulfed by a cryptoporticus of pepperino and stucco adorned with moss-covered nymphs, behind which the visitor passes as through a curtain of water. The effect is wonderful to experience and incredible to behold. Above the arcade is a small artificial porous stone hill from which a cascade flowed to the oval base; in the central grotto of the hill over the cascade is a sixteenth-century statue of Albunea, the Tybertine sibyl, with her son, flanked by the local river gods Anio and Erculaneo, whose waters flow through the villa. Surmounting all is the Fountain of Pegasus, now practically hidden, in accord with the myth of creation of the Fountain of the Muses on Parnassus.

A grotto dedicated to Diana lay in the terrace below the large arcaded belvedere that served as an outdoor dining loggia, one of a series of superimposed grottoes set into the upper hillside. Flanked by caryatids, the grotto is lavishly wrought with stucco reliefs representing scenes of metamorphoses; fragments of majolica tiles are visible, but the statues of gods and amazons have long since been removed. Grottoes within the villa proper include the wall fountain with dripping cascade in the ground story dining room.[35] The rustic fountain embellished with a sleeping Venus above the water basin—voluptuously pleasing as befits the choice of Hercules—served as a passageway to the secret garden, the private retreat for the cardinal and the inhabitants of the villa.

Homage to Venus is rendered, too, in the villa's cloister, which was once part of a Benedictine monastery on the site. Within the atrium is a triumphal fountain arch harboring a marble sleeping Venus set against a woodland grove; a Roman sarcophagus functions as a fount. Leaving the villa and descending to the town, we soon realize that grottoes are part of the vernacular. The town's wall fountains testify to this, but even more so do the geological formations and the cascades in the surrounding landscape.

Bagnaia was cited by Scamozzi and Rabasco as one of the "luoghi celebratissimi," together with Pratolino, Caprarola, and Tivoli—sites of the villas epitomizing Renaissance garden design.[36] The Villa Lante was a former hunting park in a town that was once the country residence of the bishops of Viterbo. Cardinal Gambara laid out its gardens during the years 1568-78; they were completed by Cardinal Montalto after Gambara's death in 1587. Here the uses of water manifest themselves in so many ways—the grand water chain, the small island, the cascades and jets of various orders, and so on—that the two pavilion-grottoes within visually may seem the least exciting of the garden's features. Their site, however, on either side of the fountain at the very apex of the garden's central axis, affirms their significance in the total iconographical scheme. Known as the Houses of the Muses, these classical porticoes with their rough stone lateral facades and Palladian motifs frame the large naturalistic Fountain of the Deluge, from which water supplied by the park reservoir cascades to the fountains and pool below. This grotto at the summit is in direct contrast with the intensely ordered geometric scheme below, the whole constituting a world in which nature has been manipulated by art—with the most extraordinary results.[37]

At the Villa Lante, the exedra of the Fountain of Pegasus is set against the wooded hillside in a position comparable to that of the Pegasus high above the Oval Fountain at Tivoli. Indeed, Pegasus, the winged steed who generated the Fountain of the Muses on Mount Helicon, is a popular Renaissance fountain motif, as witness Jacopo Zucchi's *Design for a Fountain* executed in the second half of the sixteenth century. In this rustic fountain design, whose subject is the Birth of Coral, Pegasus figures prominently as the triumphant mount of Perseus, who displays the head of Medusa beneath a stalactitic rock formation enriched by fragments of coral. Separate branches of the rare mineral are raised by the Nereids who stand within and about the sarcophagus forming part of the fountain's design. In its amalgam of sculptural and iconographical elements the design recalls the Medici fountains in the Castello and Boboli grottoes.[38]

In terms of hydraulic wonders, the fountains and grottoes of Pratolino are surely the apogee. Sung by Tasso, praised by Montaigne, described in detail by Francesco de' Vieri, and illustrated by Stefano della Bella, the grottoes of Pratolino stunned visitors from its earliest days until its destruction in the nineteenth century. Situated between Florence and Prato, the villa was begun in 1569 and completed in 1589 by Duke Francesco de' Medici, son of Cosimo, as a paradise for his beloved, Bianca Cappello, whom he wed in 1579, and as an expression of his scientific interests. Bernardo Sgrilli who wrote about Pratolino in 1742 tells us that Buontalenti, its architect-engineer

34. Pratolino, villa. Grotto of Pan and Fame, 1569–1589, B. Buontalenti. Etching by S. della Bella, ca. 1650, from B. Sgrilli, *Descrizione
della Reggia Villa . . . Pratolino*, Florence, 1742.

and artist of metamorphoses and illusion, "use[d] all his five senses to
embellish it."[39] Among the earliest visitors, Fynes Moryson in 1594 writes of
"a Cave under the earth leading three miles to the Fountaine of water, from
whence by many pipes the waters are brought to serve the workes of these
Gardens. . . ." He singles out for praise "these Fountaines . . . wrought
within little houses, which house is vulgarly called grotta, that is Cave (or
Den) yet they are not built under the earth but above in the manner of a
Cave."[40] The grottoes were viewed by all as a "series of *tableaux vivants* within
artificially enclosed environments."[41]

Not unexpectedly, Montaigne was astonished and amazed by the waterworks, the "thousand reservoirs, . . . [the] innumerable earthen pipes." He
writes with wonder of the

> marvel of a grotto with many niches and rooms; this part exceeds anything
> we ever saw elsewhere. It is formed and all crusted over with a certain material
> which they say is brought from some particular mountain, and they have joined
> it together with invisible nails. . . . By a single movement the whole grotto is
> filled with water, and all the seats squirt up water to your backside; and if you
> fly from the grotto . . . it may let loose a thousand jets of water from every two
> steps of that staircase. . . .[42]

Grottoes are, indeed, ubiquitous at Pratolino, both in front of the palace
and within. A prominent position is given to the personification of the River
Mugnone "which gives water to all those fountains (in the park below)"
situated at the southern approach "under the stairs at the head of
the . . . avenue."[43] An etching by Stefano della Bella represents two views of
the interior of the Grotto of Pan and Fame. At one end of the oblong room is
the figure of Fame, a hydraulic automaton flapping her wings and sounding a
golden trumpet. Below, a figure extends a cup to a thirsty dragon who bends
to drink. At the opposite end, Pan in turn plays his pipes, rests, stands,
moves, and is seated, while at the same time Syrinx is transformed into a

48

35. Pratolino, villa. Colossal statue, the *Apennino*, Giambologna. Etching by S. della Bella, ca. 1650, from B. Sgrilli, *Descrizione della Reggia Villa . . . Pratolino*, Florence, 1742.

reed.[44] Receding flagstones create a perspective on the pavement that is enhanced by the illusionistic landscapes painted beyond. The architecture serves as a proscenium arch: the stage is set for the action, which will literally be put into play by the *fontanieri*. Gualterotti, in a contemporary poem celebrating the marriage of Francesco and Bianca Cappello in 1579 said of Pratolino that in "its every grace [it] presents Art and Nature together in competition. . . "; this ravishing site once cited by Francesco de Vieri as a "place for wild nature, surrounded by mountains and full of woods."[45]

Descriptions of visitors and illustrations enable us to envision how these gardens appeared when in their glory. Their ruin began early; said an English visitor in 1754, "Pratolino has had its day."[46] Today, Giambologna's *Apennino* is one of the few surviving testaments to the villa's illustrious past. The colossus of the Apennines, a personification of the mountains to the north, is depicted as he applies pressure to a monstrous figure, who thereby gushes forth water to fill the pool below. The interior of the waterworks was once divided into "rooms in which are painted all the mines and men who dig from them metals and stones."[47] But the Golden Age, alas, has passed and none of these wall paintings survive.

Buontalenti emerges as the foremost inventor of grottoes in Italy. It was he who engineered and designed the court festivals and *intermezzi* that were in reality paeans to the grand dukes. According to Baldinucci, Buontalenti's hydraulic contrivances provided models for "all those who afterwards worked in similar things throughout all of Europe."[48] It has been shown that the history of the court spectacle is closely allied to developments in stage mechanics, and we can, therefore, assume that the grottoes and automata Buontalenti created for Pratolino sparked developments in Renaissance theatrical stagecraft.[49]

De Vieri's work, cited above, provides an exegesis in allegorical terms on the garden as an earthly paradise; like the *intermezzi*, it is symbolic of man's power to control the physical universe. Designed for the occasion of the mar-

49

riage of the Grand Duke Ferdinand de' Medici and Christina of Lorraine, niece of Catherine de' Medici, the 1589 *intermezzi* reflected a synthesis of instrumental music, song, dance, and scenic effects in the antique mode and were replete with Platonic allusions. They constitute a turning point in the history of theatre and a prelude to Baroque design, indeed, to true opera. In these *intermezzi* music was interwoven with archaeological concerns, for their object was the glorification of the power of music through the free use of antique exemplars. In the first one, *The Harmony of the Spheres,* for instance, the dazzling mise-en-scène is in accord with Platonic cosmology.[50] The infernal scene for the fourth intermezzo, *The Music of Hell,* was a fantastic yet rigidly symmetrical rockscape of subterranean passages. Its narrative contains divers episodes: the apparition of Circe on her chariot drawn by dragons; the chorus wafting above on a cloud, almost like a fragment of a heavenly body; the earth opening on infernal regions; and the dance of demons and furies.[51]

Court festivities reached a climax on this occasion, and the magnificent entertainments celebrating the marriage lasted over a month. Among the most splendid was surely the grand *naumachia* in the courtyard of the Pitti Palace, which was marked by elaborate allegorical themes that disguised the political realities of the Medici court.[52] Like the courtyards at the Villa Giulia and the Villa Imperiale at Pesaro, the Pitti court itself emphasizes the relationship between the villa and the theatre; here the gardens are above and even beyond the eye level of the spectator in the courtyard. The court's odd rusticity provides an appropriate aura of fantasy and functions as a transition from the heavily fortified aspect of the town facade to the extraordinary and artful Boboli Gardens beyond. The architecturally ordered scenography greets us upon entrance. Exactly opposite, beneath the terrace surmounted by a grand artichoke fountain, the facade is composed of an arcade of five bays, whose niches are adorned with fountains and Roman statues of Her-

36. *Inferno*, design for *Intermezzo*, 1589. Drawing by B. Buontalenti. Paris, Louvre.

50

37. Florence, Pitti Palace. Court. Engraving by G. A. Böckler, *Architectura curiosa nova*, Nuremberg, 1664.

38. Bormarzo, Sacra Bosco. *Gate of Hell*, ca. 1550–1570.

cules. The centerpiece divulges its treasures gradually: within the arch is the seventeenth-century Grotto of Moses, its vault decorated with grotesques. The grand porphyry statue of the lawgiver to whom the principal virtues are attributed is accompanied by personifications of Law, Empire, Clemency, and Zeal, all surrounding an elliptical pool with bathing putti, who barely emerge from the now stagnant waters.

Survival of the Grotesque

Strange as it may seem we are still ill informed about the genesis of the most grotesque of all Renaissance gardens, the park created by Pier Francesco Orsini at Bormarzo. Perhaps it is because today the gardens are so overgrown with dense shrubbery and vines that the monstrous denizens within are hardly visible. Among the most compelling of these rough stone figures is the Ogre, the upper lip of whose gaping jaws bears the inscription "Ogni pensiero vo . . . ." ("Every thought flies."), surely inspired by Dante's telling words in his *Divine Comedy*, "All hope abandon ye who enter here." The word Ogre itself is a variation of Orcus, one of the names of the King of Hell (and of a river associated with the orc, that most voracious of cetaceans, the killer whale). Here, the entry leads to no garden but to a large subterranean world, its white stone bench and table recalling a Mithraic chapel, or even more likely the domain of Pluto.[53] Whatever the meaning of the sombre and overgrown landscape, it yet eloquently bespeaks the irrational side of Renaissance ratio.

Dissemination in France: Imitations and Innovations

Turning to France, we find evidence of a strong native tradition in the realm of the grotto—another instance of the survival of antique modes. Villard de Hon-

51

39. Fontainebleau. Grotte des Pins, 1541–1543. Engraving by A. Fantuzzi, 1545.

necourt's notebooks evoke this ancient art in illustrations of automata. Many of these devices were derived from examples created by Alexandrian inventors and known in Arab manuscripts and were used by the French court for the sole purpose of entertainment.[54] In the 1440s-50s Duke Philip the Good lavished great expense on the mechanical contrivances in his castle at Hesdin in Artois. A vivid account of these practical jokes is given in the inventory of payments for these curiosities, mechanisms placed along the wall that "squirt water in so many places that nobody in the gallery could possibly save himself from getting wet. . . ."[55]

Although the development of the grotto occurs more or less at the same time in France and Italy, the invention and revival of the classical form, like all things Renaissance, really belong to Italy. The rustic style is developed by Serlio in Book IV of his treatise on architecture published in 1537 and dedicated to Francis I. This treatise was a prelude to Serlio's arrival at Fontainebleau as "architect in ordinance for the King's buildings." What Serlio brought to France was certainly gleaned from the art of the followers of Raphael, particularly that of Giulio Romano as manifested in the Palazzo del Te. It is this *mode d'Italie* that Primaticcio or one of his compatriots incorporated into the Grotte des Pins at Fontainebleau , that bastion of Italianism newly formed on French soil.[56]

Time has not favored the grottoes in France, about which we know little from first hand observation. Of sixteenth-century grottoes, the only significant survivors in a fairly intact state are those at Fontainebleau and at La Bastie d'Urfé.[57] The former is a magnificent example of the forces of nature versus those of art, its stone Atlantes seeming to erupt from a primordial preternatural existence while guarding the entrance to the wonders within. In the *di sotto in su* illusionistic roundels, Juno and Minerva must have presided over a wondrous aggregate of fountains and pools reflecting the splendor of their surroundings, but regrettably they are all gone now. Located beneath the Gallery of Ulysses

52

40. *The Banquet of Acheloos* (?), 1547. Pen and ink and wash drawing by L. Penni, 1547, Munich, Collection H. List.

and adjacent to the Pavilion of Pomona, it is tempting to ascribe a Homeric iconography to the decor here. Do the boundary figures of Pan and Syrinx suggest a dedication to Pan? Recondite mythological associations are almost infinite when delving within the precincts of Fontainebleau. Fortunately, what time has destroyed, art has preserved. The *Banquet of Acheloos* engraved by Lucca Penni, one of the Italian followers of Raphael at Fountainebleau, depicts a stalactitic subterranean chamber; the story here told is probably set according to Ovid (*Met.* 8.547ff) in the cave of the river-god Acheloos "built of porous pumice and rough tufa stone. The ground . . . damp with soft moss, the ceiling roofed with alternate bands of conch shells and shells of purple fish . . ." with barefoot nymphs attending the banquet table. The print like the story of Acheloos itself is pure invention, but its roots are undoubtedly closer to the banquet of Tiberius in the grotto of Sperlonga than to the "modern" reality of the Grotte des Pins.[58]

Surely, too, the dichotomy between art and nature is dramatized in the irregularity and the rustic quality of the grotto within the supremely regular and geometric Renaissance garden. It may be understood as the expression of the irrational in a superbly rational world, the element of chance in a highly planned cosmos, the notion of chaos within the ordered scheme. The domain of the nymphs has been transformed into a realm where Renaissance monarchs could contemplate ideas of ancient glory and resurrect the past in their own images. This is the height of recondite art, only paralleled in the programs of the Italian grottoes in the gardens of the Medici princes at Castello, Boboli, and Pratolino.

La Bastie d'Urfé in Forez near Lyon, interwoven with components of L'Astrée and innumerable signs of Neoplatonic syncretism, manifests an opposing architectural system. The pastoral novel written by Honoré d'Urfé, grandson of Claude who built the château, reflects much of the arcadian sentiment of which the grotto partakes. Here the exterior forms a discrete part of the château, while the flights of fancy can only be experienced on the interior. Ad-

41. Forez, La Bastie d'Urfé. Grotto, 1551.

joining a chapel, the grotto acts as a narthex, a place for physical cleansing (for "baptism") as implied in the inscription on the entry, "Mens sana in corpore sano." The combination of grotto and museum as exemplified by Isabella d'Este's studiolo-grotto for the Palace of Mantua is, in a sense, repeated here in the proximity of the grotto to the library above.

In a similiar fashion, the grotto at Meudon, a veritable museum, contains the antiquities collection of the Cardinal de Lorraine. An inscription on the facade between busts of Plato and Aristotle consecrated the place "to the Muses of Henri II." Ironically, while the extraordinary marvels of the interior are always praised, only views of the exterior built into the terraced slopes overlooking the Seine remain. Ronsard's *Chant pastoral* of 1559 celebrating the marriage of the Duke of Lorraine to Claude of France, and set in the architectural confines of the grotto, seems to echo a Pythagorean ritual, discussed by Plotinus in his *Life of Pythagoras:* "[D]escending in the so-called cave of Ida, he passes three times nine days according to the ritual; he offers Zeus a funerary sacrifice, and learns secrets concerning the gods. . . ."[59] This type of grotto is extended in size in the seventeenth century as can be seen in Marot's engraving with the caption "grotto" and in the terraced slopes of St. Germain-en-Laye. These examples are far indeed from our preconceived notions of what a grotto should be and even further from any idea of the grotesque.

That the cult of nymphs was popular at mid-century can be seen in the poems of the Pléiade and in the magnificent *Fontaine des Innocents*, that paradigm of French classicism erected in the heart of Paris in 1549 to mark the entry of Henri II into the city. Shortly thereafter in 1560, Poldo d'Albenas, discoursing on the antiquities of Nîmes, wrote of the old Roman fountain sanctuary consecrated to the god Nemausus. This grand nymphaeum in the manner of the Fountain Egeria had been founded on the site of a perennial source of water.[60] Originally built in the time of Augustus, it was set within a barrel-vaulted hall, "one of the most impressive, but also most problematic Roman buildings in

42. Meudon. Grotto, 1552–1560, Primaticcio, etc. Engraving by A. Perelle, from *Veues des belles maisons de France*, Paris, ca. 1650.

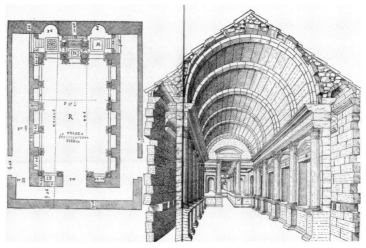

43. Nîmes. Nymphaeum. Plan and view. Woodcut in J. Poldo d'Albenas, *Discours historial de l'antique et illustre cité de Nimes*, Lyon, 1560.

Gaul."[61] The ruins we see today near the second-century Temple of Diana (probably once part of the Baths) are set within a delightful park built in the eighteenth century.

Another antique type, of a form relatively rare in France, is the cryptoporticus of the Château of Anet designed by Philibert Delorme. Erected as a memorial to Diane de Poitier's deceased husband, Louis de Brèze, the château is renowned for its subtle allusions to the mistress of Henri II. The crypt is no exception. As has been noted, the crescent formed by the flight of stairs connecting the château to the garden, alludes to the crescent moon, one attribute of the lunar aspect of the goddess Diane. The crypt's complex vaulting system served as a retaining wall for the château and as a passage to the garden.

55

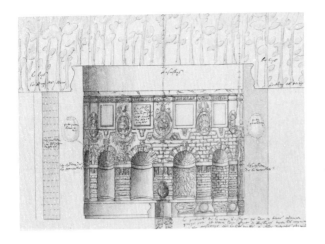

44. Tuileries. *Design for a Rustic Grotto*, 1567–1570. Pen and ink and wash drawing attributed to B. Palissy. Paris, Bibliothèque Nationale.

Aside from its debt to antique and High Renaissance precedents such as the Villa Belvedere and the Villa Madama, the whole is a tribute to the genius of Delorme.[62]

But beyond a doubt it is Palissy, "inventor of the King's rustic potteries" and ardent Huguenot, who was the creator of the most spectacular sixteenth-century grottoes in France. Unfortunately, only fragments of his work in this sphere survive and a sole drawing in the Destailleur Collection, which has been attributed to him. The latter is an elevation of a rustic grotto and may be a study for the grotto designed for the gardens in Catherine de' Medici's new Tuileries Palace. This grotto had a brilliantly enameled interior and was situated on an island approached via a bridge. Some idea of the appearance of Palissy's grottoes may be gleaned from his ceramics but far more may be understood by perusing the detailed descriptions of the many grottoes he was planning for the Queen and for the Connétable Anne de Montmorency.[63] The Museum of Ferrante Imperato in Naples and the *Wunderkammern* of the Germans, with their collections of objects of art and the fossilized matter and curiosities of natural history, seem analogous in spirit to these fantasies of Palissy.[64] It might be intriguing to explore the Florentine Medicean grottoes in terms of those of Catherine in France.

Ernst Kris, discussing this most prolific grotto maker, Palissy, points out that Palissy's view of nature is as old as that of Pliny.[65] Both hold to the formula "Natura Artis Magistra." Though unsung in the annals of art, Palissy has been compared to Rabelais as representative of the new search for a knowledge in which the direct observation of natural phenomena is uppermost, a knowledge based on empirical research rather than on a priori constructs.[66] In fact, Palissy's preface to the *Discours Admirable,* written in 1580, has been cited as being on the same path Francis Bacon would later tread. But Palissy is no ordinary naturalist, pragmatist, or political outcast. As a master of the mystical and the mystifying, the philosopher Gaston Bachelard finds Palissy a fit subject for his chapter "Shells" in *The Poetics of Space*. Bachelard postulates that the shell must be a "subject for infinite meditation" for a potter or enamelist. Shells were indeed a source of natural inspiration for Palissy whether in his plans for a fortress city or in the chambers he designed for gardens as places of retreat. To ac-

56

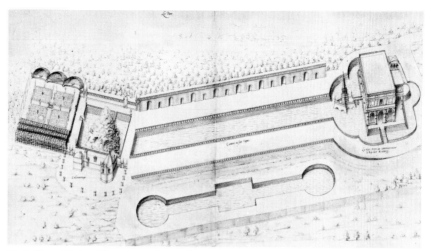

45. Gaillon. Maison Blanche, *rocher* and hermitage, 1556. Engraving by J. A. Du Cerceau the Elder, *Les Plus Excellents Bastiments de France*, Paris, 1576–1579.

centuate the natural character of the chamber—its enameled interior, "a cave in the form of a coiled shell"—he had it covered with earth "so that having planted several trees in the aforesaid earth, it would not seem to have been built."[67] Perhaps this subterranean "home" in the shell of a rock was an appropriate dream for an avowed Huguenot in his quest for solitude—and protection.

Psalm 104 (10-13), a hymn to God celebrating the Creation, together with the *Hypnerotomachia Poliphili* are acknowledged by Palissy to be the sources of those idiosyncratic and rustic herm pilasters that appear to go beyond the excesses of Fontainebleau. Among the many grotto types he invented or utilized was the *rocher* planned for Chenonceau, a type reflected in festival decor as well as in gardens. We are reminded of the addition to Gaillon under the auspices of Cardinal Charles de Bourbon where the natural surroundings of the Maison Blanche—the canal; the *rocher*, or hermitage; and the adjacent *clos*, park, and distant view—provided a perfect setting for pastorals with bucolic allusions.[68] This amalgam of theatre/festival hall and retreat (the latter a cave of Muses with its own vineyard or cloister) echoes those retreats found in Hadrian's Villa or in the Domus Aurea. Dubbed the "Parnassus of Gaillon" by Charles IX, the *rocher* is included as part of other monuments to the Muses. In fact, it becomes a fairly common theatrical prop. Jean Dorat's 1575 festival book describing the Ballet of the Provinces of France illustrates an elaborate *rocher*, its arches and rustic niches adorned with fair court damsels who descend like nymphs to perform the dance.[69] All this was only one aspect of the programs staged by Catherine de' Medici in the Tuileries Gardens to entertain the Polish ambassadors. These designs are known to us via the Valois tapestries installed in the Uffizi Gallery. Gardens, like politics, were subject to the Medici connection.

Aside from a few notable developments such as the complex at Gaillon, forays in the relatively frivolous art of grotto making had to await the end of the century. Usually associated with the seventeenth century, the grotto of Noisy-le-Roi near Versailles was built circa 1582-99 and is known largely through

57

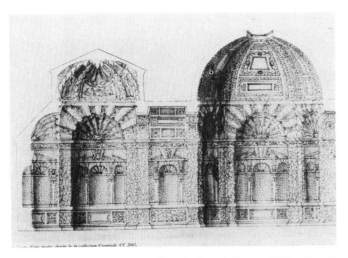

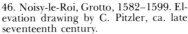

46. Noisy-le-Roi, Grotto, 1582–1599. Elevation drawing by C. Pitzler, ca. late seventeenth century.

47. The Salle de Bourbon, Grotto of Pan. Engraving in B. de Beaujoyeulx, *Le Ballet comique de la Reyne*, 1582.

Marot's engravings and a sketch by Pitzler. Destroyed in 1732, the grotto was the principal ornament of the garden at the entry of the park. Of the casino-type, it included within an octagonal salon with vaulted dome a buffet of *rocaille* and a fountain table.[70] We learn of this extraordinary grotto from an unpublished manuscript that speaks of "its figures in low relief representing Neptune and Thetis; *rocaille* and shells in one-hundred different ways form compartments of charming mosaics. Niches of *rocaille* with . . . Tritons and Sirens which imitate nature, millions of small black round stones, aquatic birds, dolphins, jetting water and frescoed walls. . . ."[71] The mode was Italian; no expense was spared. Other sources imply that the Noisy grotto was a preferred haunt of Louis XIII, then the six-year-old dauphin, who is recorded as playing there in 1607. That the grotto harbored more serious activities, specifically a literary salon, is revealed in a letter of Estienne Pasquier of 1591 and a poem, *Le Séjour de Dyctinne et des muses. À Madame la Mareschalle de Retz,* whose verses reveal midst fountains, arbors, and babbling brooks the presence of Diane in the person of the patroness, Madame de Retz.[72]

Henri IV's accession to the throne in 1594 was marked by the construction of vast urban schemes in Paris. Just outside the city, the gardens of St. Germain-en-Laye were enlarged, their terraced slopes incorporating the new technological wonders gleaned from Italy and often, through a medieval lens, from antiquity. As with gardens, so too with grottoes. From the private garden retreat of humanist villas — the *locus amoenus* (delightful place) resurrected from the texts of Pliny and the ancients, the Renaissance popes and princes soon looked toward rustic settings to enhance their collections of classical sculpture. The intricate aquatic tableaux thus created became descendants of the marvelous fountains and automata popular in courts and gardens from imperial Rome to Byzantium and the medieval world. A counterpart to animate the rigid geometry of the Renaissance garden, the grotto could be construed as a natural or an artificial entity. Amid the ambiguity, illusion reigned.

V. Worlds of Fancy: The Baroque Spectacle

> Now in the same measure that spirits enter the cavities of the brain they also leave them and enter the pores [or conduits] in its substance, and from these conduits they proceed to the nerves. And depending on their entering . . . some nerves rather than others, they are able to change the shapes of the muscles into which these nerves are inserted and in this way to move all the members. Similarly you may have observed in the grottoes and fountains in the gardens of our kings that the force that makes the water leap from its source is able of itself to move divers machines and even to make them play certain instruments. . .according to various arrangements of the tubes through which the water is conducted.
>
> René Descartes, *Treatise of Man*, 1629.[1]

Theatres of Illusion

By the end of the sixteenth century, imitation had given way to illusion, fact to fancy, truth to deception. Nature had been surpassed by both art and science. The conquest of space on a two-dimensional surface, the proliferation of knowledge as evidenced in encyclopedias devoted to geology and botany and in scientific and philosophical treatises paved the way for a new type of garden art. This is the world of Shakespeare, Corneille, and Racine; of the operas of Peri, Monteverdi, and Cavalli; of the masques of Inigo Jones, Ben Jonson, and the Stuart court. Theatrical spectacles and festivals, born in the sixteenth century, often serving as court allegories or as morality plays, appear in a new guise. Now the main goal is to arouse wonder, to introduce the element of suspense, to elicit surprise or even fear—above all to astonish the observer. New advances in mathematics made these wonders possible. This is the great age of hydraulic research in the wake of Leonardo's experiments; it is the time of Galileo, Toricelli, Descartes, Pascal, and Newton.

Predictably, the grotto was a common element in theatrical scenery.[2] The arch of the cave echoes a proscenium arch and provides the frame for the drama within. Note, for example, Carew's instructions for Inigo Jones's *Design for a Proscenium Arch:* "At this [the end of the masque] the under part of the Roche opens, and out of a Cave are seen to come the Masquers. . . ."[3]

59

48. Prologue for *Andromède* by P. Corneille. Engraving by F. Chauveau, 1650.

49. St. Germain-en-Laye. Bird's eye view, 1599–1610. Engraving after T. Francini, 1614.

Both grotto and stage enclose isolated spectacles; both may furnish rapid changes of scene to surprise the spectator.[4] Giacomo Torelli's theatrical designs, made in mid-seventeenth-century Venice, utilize the theme of the grotto, and such designs as Chauveau's engraving for the Prologue in the first illustrated edition of Corneille's *Andromède* are also in this genre.[5]

Like the theatre, the grotto thus becomes the perfect realm of fantasy, the domain of illusion. It is an ideal vehicle for the seventeenth-century fusion of the arts. And in a more practical way, the grotto, like the rock or mountain, the tree or fountain, becomes a standard topos in the garden and park as it does in the theatre and court.[6]

Under Henri IV and Louis XIII, the grottoes of St. Germain-en-Laye, the royal domain, became one of the principal attractions of the gardens. Designed by the Francini, the Florentine hydraulic engineers who would later work on the gardens of Fontainebleau and Versailles, these grottoes were built between 1589 and 1609 on a series of terraces laid out by Henri IV and Etienne Dupérac.[7] Exteriors that meshed with the landscape opened to reveal a rustic ambiance of *rocaille* and shells simulating maritime grottoes. Let us glance at the grotto of Orpheus with its beasts above and along the sides, the birds seeming to flap their wings and the trees to move in time to the harmony of the divine chorus.[8] Let us look, too, at the grotto of Perseus as depicted by Abraham Bosse, wherein the shells of the walls are arranged in the form of satyrs, sea monsters, and birds. In this marvelous place, grotesque figures suddenly jetted streams of water to the surprise of visitors and the joy of the young Louis XIII—it is the triumph of technology and invention over more rational artistic concepts. How unlike Versailles, where the mechanics would be used exclusively for the enhancement of art and the glorification of the king.

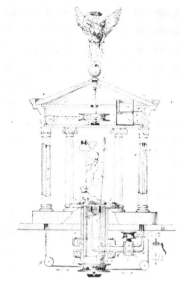

50. Orpheus Grotto. Engraving in S. De Caus, *Les Raisons des forces mouvantes*, Paris, 1624

51. Automaton, mobile theatre according to Hero, *Automata*. In A. Chapuis and E. Droz, *Les Automates*, Neuchatel, 1949.

Wonders of Water

During the baroque period, the emphasis in gardens and grottoes was on sheer artifice: nature was to be surpassed by scenography, *ars* wedded to *scientia*. The grotto became a theatre for ingenious displays of waterworks and one of the designer's overriding concerns became the conquest of mechanical difficulties. The daring of waterworks and the plays generated by varying combinations of jets and sprays were unparalleled at this time.

Because little survives of these early seventeenth-century grottoes, we must turn to the legacy of Salomon De Caus for an idea of their appearance. Following his countryman and fellow Huguenot, Bernard Palissy, whose main contribution in this area was his written works, De Caus has bequeathed to us graphic data as well.[9] As an hydraulic engineer, he used pumps invented by Ctesibius and drew on the experiments with water clocks and pneumatic organs and the application of the pump to a water jet as described in the treatises of Hero and Vitruvius. De Caus diagramed the instruments often hidden within the grotto and noted the way in which the sense of motion may be reversed by the play of counterweights, valves, and steam, as was accomplished in those Roman musical devices propelled by water wheels.[10] But it was only in the Renaissance, with the revival of antique myths, that these mechanical wonders proliferated in the garden. In developing technical amusements for the court based on the manipulation of water, De Caus drew on humanist translations of the learned commentaries of Archimedes, Euclid, and Hero (the latter translated into Italian in Urbino in 1560) and the treatises of Vitruvius and Pliny. Here is a revival of hydraulics like those

61

used in the grotto-theatre of the ancients. De Caus was influenced by the automata and the water organs constructed by Hero of Alexandria, a disciple of Ctesibius, whose writings on pneumatics, mechanics, water clocks, and applications of the siphon had just been translated; he read, too, the works of Philo of Byzantium, where water was used as a motor force to produce mechanical combinations of picturesque, amusing, and instructive effects, and also works of tenth-century Constaninople. In the *Pneumatica*, Hero employs human, animal, and architectural forms in order to give readers a better understanding of the laws of applied physics. His treatise, *Automata,* speaks of a mobile theatre, in which hydraulic conduits were hidden in the capitals, columns, and pediment; these mechanisms set in motion the figure of Victory at the summit and the figures of dancing bacchantes beating their cymbals and tambours below.[11] These ancient automata survive in the work of Arab scientists in the early Middle Ages. Al-Jazari's treatise, 1204-06, demonstrates water-lifting devices for "fountains and perpetual flutes."[12] Such Muslim inventions spread to Spain and Sicily and eventually to Western Europe, where they flourished once more in the early fourteenth-century gardens of the château of Hesdin for the Dukes of Burgundy, and in the castles of Pavia and Milan for the Visconti rulers.[13]

In the course of his Italian trip in 1595, which included visits to Tivoli, Frascati, and Pratolino, De Caus became acquainted with Heinrich Schickhart, the architect of Duke Frederick of Wurtenberg in Stuttgart. Schickhart's account of his Italian journey contains vivid descriptions of grottoes as mythological or allegorical *tableaux*, in particular, of the waterworks of Pratolino and other Italian villas.[14] De Caus is recorded to have made sketches in 1599 of several hydraulic machines by Buontalenti, the architect of Pratolino. That there was a relationship between the two is therefore quite probable.

While in the service of the Tuscan Medici Duke Ferdinand I in 1597, De Caus had witnessed the first opera, *Daphne,* by Peri and Cascini. He was so impressed by the spectacle that when he was summoned to work in the Palatinate gardens in Heidelberg, there arose visions of creating a German Florence on the Neckar. Frederick V provided the opportunity in 1613, when he decided to embellish the castle at Heidelberg in honor of the marriage of the last of the elector princes to Elizabeth, daughter of James I. *Hortus Palatinus,* published in Frankfurt in 1615-20 and dedicated to Frederick V, is a testimony to the garden designed by De Caus, which unfortunately remained incompleted due to the outbreak of the Thirty Years War in 1618.

Perhaps it was the difficult sloping terrain of the terrace, set as it was against the mountainside, that led De Caus to fill it with grottoes in the Italian manner similar to those in the French gardens at Meudon, St. Germain-en-Laye, and later at Vaux. Instead of a true Italian garden, however, we see a collection of gardens "without any uniformity."[15] Neither waterworks, nor grottoes are treated systematically. We are still within a medieval frame where attention is riveted on separate elements rather than on the whole. Grottoes are everywhere — in the walls of the upper terrace, in the corners of the garden, opposite the entrance to the palace. Today, amid the splendid

52. Heidelberg, perspective view of gardens by S. De Caus, *Hortus Palatinus*. Engraving by M. Merian, Frankfurt, 1620.

53. Heidelberg, gardens of the Palatinate. Grotto with river god. Actual state.

pseudo-Roman ruins and terrace gardens perched high above the Neckar, fragments of the grottoes may be discerned. The grand grotto in the southeast corner of the mid-level, once profusely decorated with sparkling shells and streams of jetting water, is now but a dark shadowy cave with a decaying river god, Neptune, placed before it.

We learn more about De Caus's grottoes from his *Les Raisons des forces mouvantes avec diverses machines tant utiles que plaisantes.* Published in Frankfurt in 1615, the book was dedicated to Louis XIII.[16] Many of the grottoes described in the work are miniature theatres that recall the scenery of Florentine operatic performances and *intermezzi*. The myths, too, are similar: Acis and Galatea, Echo and Narcissus, the grotto of Neptune and his entourage, Daphne, Orpheus and Eurydice; other subjects stress the mechanics, as the nymph playing an organ to which an echo responds, and above all, the Grotto

63

54. Heidelberg. *Neptune Grotto with Rotating Machine*. Etching in S. De Caus, *Les Raisons des forces mouvantes*, Paris, 1624.

of Torches, whose transformation scenes have been compared to a court ballet.[17] De Caus's works at Heidelberg are difficult to decipher, but it has been assumed that at least some of the "Problems" presented in *Les Raisons* were executed for the gardens there.[18]

Theory and Design

De Caus's younger brother, Isaac, continued his work in both theory and practice. His 1644 publication, *Nouvelles Inventions de lever l'eau plus haut que sa source, 1644,* is literally lifted from Salomon's *Forces mouvantes . . .* , its theory on water conduits based largely on Archimedes.[19] Isaac laid out the formal rectangular garden at Wilton House, Wiltshire, between 1649-53. Situated at the very end of the garden, the grotto is the main focus of the central axis. Its triple triumphal arch seems to prefigure Louis XIV's grotto at Versailles. An English traveler, Celia Fiennes, displays a naive delight in describing the water effects, "toys" and "freak jets" that "wett the strangers... [and] figures... that can weep water on the beholders...."[20]

When the ninth Earl of Pembroke began remodeling the landscape of Wilton in 1732, he substituted a garden in the style of Kent for the formal garden of De Caus. But in its day Wilton Garden was "esteem'd the noblest in England" by the diarist, John Evelyn, and its grotto deemed "the finest and most charming . . . I remember ever hearing and seeing" by the astronomer, Christian Huygens.[21] In 1688 John Woolridge wrote that this grotto was "the most famous of this kind that this Kingdom affords . . . on which no cost was spared to make it compleat, and wherein you may view or might have lately so done the best of waterworks. . . ."[22] In *Hortus Pembrochianus,* by Isaac De Caus, the interior and exterior of the grotto are presented on one plate. We see Triton blowing his conch, Venus and Cupid borne through the waters on a shell, the river gods and goddesses, the large reserve of water for the grotto noted above.[23] The tunes are straight out of Isaac De Caus — the "melody of

55. Wiltshire, Wilton House. Grotto interior. Drawing by I. De Caus, *Hortus Pembrochianus*, ca. 1647.

56. Bedfordshire, Woburn Abbey. Grotto, ca. 1627. Attributed to I. De Caus.

Nightingerlls and all sorts of birds" was simulated by means of the movement of water and air.[24]

On the occasion of the Prince's Twelfth Night Masque, Inigo Jones and Ben Jonson presented at Whitehall Banqueting House *The Fortunate Isles and Their Union.* The scene "Neptune's Triumph" has as its mise-en-scène a Palladian type street with a row of two-storied buildings on each side receding into the aqueous distance. Each rusticated arch is guarded by caryatid termes à la Fontainebleau; its terraces are adorned with conch-blowing tritons. Thus Inigo transfers the Italian garden to the stage.[25] The grotto was built when the fourth Earl of Bedfordshire came to Woburn to escape the plague then raging in London. Once open, the loggia faced the sunless north; it was a cool place, and hence thought to be a healthy one.[26]

Today's visitor to Woburn moves through the crypt and vaults before ascending to the grotto. The mild shock of climbing to enter this loggia-grotto is enhanced by its close juxtaposition to the parlor. Suddenly we are in this curious room whose architectural components consist of simulated rock, which moved one visitor to exclaim, "Good gracious, that comes as a surprise, doesn't it! All shells!" Elaborate arabesque patterns of shells in concentric rows form the ribs of the vaulted ceiling and the arched niches on the side walls; lintels and lunettes delineate the latter with marvelous patterns comprised of bas-relief shell mosaics. Here are the masks of Neptune, nereids and putti riding on dolphins or leaning on a giant shell chariot, while shimmering mother-of-pearl makes the very waves seem to move. Classical elements abound: Roman statues above an attic relief of a Greek maiden, antique statues within the niches, and the pride of place given to Bacchus, who occupies the central arched niche opposite the garden window. Grapes dangling from one hand, he leans on a wood bark about which a serpent winds. Once enriched with running fountains, Walpole in 1751 called it the "Bathing Room."[27] Art is dominant in this grotto; nature could not be further removed.

57. Heidelberg, gardens of the Palatinate. *Design of a Grotto Wherein a Ball Rises by Means of the Force of Water*. Etching by S. De Caus, *Les Raisons des forces mouvantes*, Paris, 1624.

58. Enstone. Grotto, facade, and interior, 1628–1635 by T. Bushell. Engraving from R. Plot, *Natural History of Oxfordshire*, 1677.

Contemporary, and comparable, to Wilton in its water effects are the Enstone Marvels, built by a servant of Francis Bacon, Thomas Bushell. His grotto at Enstone in Oxfordshire together with its hermitage has been dated to the early 1630s. Bushell enclosed a 10 to 12 foot rock "full of cavities and hollows which dripped water" in a vaulted room in a "faire 4 square Building of Freestone" with innumerable water pipes concealed within. Bushell had a penchant for the macabre as well; he lived in the hermitage above the grotto, whose rooms were draped in black to symbolize "the melancholy retyr'd life like a Hermits."[28] Totally destroyed in the mid-nineteenth century, Enstone was in a sufficiently splendid state when viewed by Robert Plot in 1677 to spur him to write that the "waterworks . . . surpass all others of this country. . . "; here Thomas Bushell "met with a rock so wonderfully contrived by nature herself that he thought it worthy of all imaginable advancement by art."[29] On the occasion of Charles I's visit to Enstone in 1635, a visitor records the "spouts [that riseth] up about 9. foote high, a Streame which raiseth up on her top a Silver Ball, and as the sayd Streame riseth or falleth to any pitch or distance, so doth the Ball, with playing, tossing and keeping continually at the top of the sayd ascending Streame...." From this statement Roy Strong concludes that the fountain device of a ball rising and falling on a single jet of water, illustrated by Salomon De Caus, was actually executed here, as was the design of a water curtain composed of a wall of jet streams activated by the approaching spectator.[30] But again Hero has set the precedent, as we see in his *Pneumatica,* Theorem 45, which is entitled "A Jet of Steam Supporting a Sphere."[31]

Grottoes continue to be multivalent throughout the period. At Chatsworth, the so-called grotto serves more than "severall ffanceyes to make diversion."[32] Located within the house, it is really the base of a large buttress that lends support to the Elizabethan hall. Although deemed a grotto from 1689 on, it has little in common with its contemporaries, except for its stone walls, its adornments fit for a dungeon, and its general aura of gloom. But the earl decided that it would "supply all ye house with water...." Documents dated 1691-92 affirm these words of Celia Fiennes, and surely a reservoir is an appropriate function for this grottolike structure, considering its site at the base of the well that lay at the foot of the house's Great Stairs.[33]

By the end of the century, the grotto is so commonplace that it is included in John Woolridge's prescriptions for modern gardens as "a place that is capable of giving you so much pleasure and delight, that you may bestow not undeservedly what cost you please on it, by paving it with Marble or immuring it with Stone or Rock-work, either Natural or Artificially resembling the excellencies of nature."[34]

Grotto as Nymphaeum

As in ancient times, Rome is golden once more during the Baroque period. This is the age of Bernini and the wonderfully elaborate conceits that gave new dimensions to the art of creating fountains. This is also the time when nymphaea became theatres of water and even relatively modest fountains were given monumental setpieces. Seventeeth-century prints are witness to this development, depicting, for example, the fountains of Paul V constructed in 1612 to celebrate the Acqua Paola, which was to lead waters to the Vatican Hill. In the sixteenth-century museum garden, the Belvedere, antique sculpture had already been enhanced by waterworks and the Tigris and Ariadne fountains adopted grottolike settings. From their beginnings, these gardens were loci for *divertissements*, the fountains serving for display as well as for use.[35] Among the intricate artifices designed to imitate nature are the Fountain dello Scoglio or dell'Aquila of 1611-12, attributed to Carlo Maderno, and the rustic grotto-fountain of 1615, later called the Galera after the metal ship from which it seemed to rise. Venturini's engraving of the latter

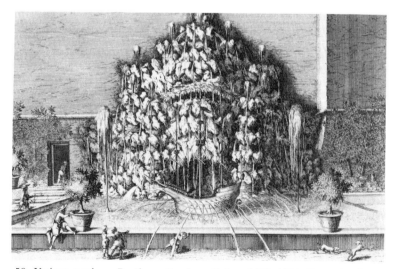

59. Vatican gardens. Rustic grotto, later *Galera*, 1613–1614. Engraving by G. F. Venturini, *Le fontane de Roma*, Rome, 1675.

67

60. Frascati, Villa Aldobrandini, Sala dei Venti, ca. 1601. Engraving by D. Barrière, 1647.

61. Frascati, Villa Aldobrandini. Cave in park.

with its well-camouflaged crowning eagle almost seems to be a pastiche of the two fountains.

Frascati—Tusculum to the ancients, site of the villas of Cicero and Pliny—is the locus of the most spectacular waterworks of all.[36] Nymphaea in the villas of Frascati became *teatri dell' acqua,* grand hemicycles with fountains and statuary within. Through these features the villas, often reconstructed on ancient foundations, acquired great fame. Their prominence and influence considerably exceed that of their sixteenth-century predecessors. The magnificent Teatro dell'Acqua at the Villa Aldobrandini, for example, has been interpreted by modern scholars as a symbol of the "new power of the Church," a *theatrum mundi* of God, and a testimony to the "noble role of man on earth."[37] Hydraulic mechanisms were used to control and manipulate nature, to simulate such natural phenomena as wind, rain, thunder, and lightning. From his vantage point in the palace, Cardinal Aldobrandini had an unobstructed view of the entire theater. Only slightly less renowned than the magnificient frontispiece designed for the Cardinal's pleasure is the Room of Parnassus, also called the *Stanza dei venti*, at the right, which is dedicated to Apollo. The central niche of the one-time dining salon, which depicts the Apollonian forces of light conquering those of darkness, contains a stucco (wood, according to Passeri) tableau representing Mount Parnassus with Apollo and the nine Muses, the whole crowned by Pegasus. It is inscribed "Hither I, Apollo, have migrated, accompanied by the Muses, here will be my Delphi, Helicon, and Delos."[38] Giovanni B. Falda, the seventeenth-century engraver known for his views of Rome, notes the many water zones with pleasant and tricky curiosities, the lyre and wind instruments played by all, and the organ under the mount. This is the grotto-room described by Evelyn wherein "rises a copper ball that continually daunces about 3 foote above the pavement by virtue of a Wind conveyed secretely to a hole beneath it, with many devices to wett the unwary spectators. . . ."[39] The truly grotesque is reserved for the shady recesses of the park—a reminder perhaps of the dark forces of nature as yet uncontrolled by art.

62. Frascati, Villa Mondragone. Water theatre, ca. 1615, G. Fontana, Engraving in
G. B. Falda, *Le fontane di Roma*, ed. 1675–91 (?).

Of a similar genre to the Villa Aldobrandini, and almost as famous, is the
Villa Mondragone, where Gregory XIII signed the Bull reforming the calen-
dar. Few descriptions of the water theatre, created by the Roman hydraulic
engineer Giovanni Fontana, are more playful than that of Charles De Brosses
of Dijon, who visited the villa in 1739:

> The ceremony started. . . .around a—shall we say: polypriapic-basin (the
> semicircular peschiera). Its whole balustrade was fitted with a number of
> leather hoses, the thickness of a man's leg, with copper nozzles. Laxly curved in
> an indolent attitude they lay until we turned a cock. Now the air compressed by
> water swelled their hollow bodies, the charming gents became more and more
> erect and began—how does Rabelais put it—to shoot fresh water
> tirelessly. . . .[40]

Even the nymphaeum-type fountain may serve as a theatrical backdrop.
For example, the courtyard in the production of *La Finta Pazza*, 1645, may
easily be compared to the nymphaeum at Wideville. Built in 1635, the facade
of Wideville is close in style to the nymphaeum at Luxembourg, better known
as the *Fontaine Médicis*. Both share common prototypes in the triumphal arches of the grand papal fountains, in the facade of the Boboli grotto and more
distantly, in that of the Herculaneum nymphaeum. After the Revolution, the
Luxembourg grotto (perhaps by Salomon de Brosse, circa 1620) was restored
and transported from its original position to the terminus of the Allée des
Platanes, leading from the east side of the château. Personifications of the
Seine and Marne acted as volutes and in a central niche was placed a
sculpture, *Venus Emerging from Her Bath*. When, in 1861, the nymphaeum was
transformed on the garden side, Venus was deposed for the white marble
presence of Polyphemus surprising Acis and Galatea, a striking contrast to
the dark pool. In the lateral niches we see a faun and a huntress—all sculpted

69

63. Wideville, château. Nymphaeum, 1635. Facade.

64. Herculaneum. Nymphaeum of Neptune and Anfitrite, second half of first century A.D.

by Ottin (1856-59). A bas-relief representing the Fountain of Leda (1820) adorns the facade on the rue de Médicis. A large water basin was carved at the foot of the monument, but due to insufficient water, the grotto, with its prominent shield of Marie de' Medici, became primarily an imposing frontispiece. Here the entity is seen at the end of the magnificently shaded canal in a remarkably evocative photograph by Atget.[41]

Wideville was acquired in 1630 by the Superintendent of Finances, Claude de Bullion. Like the Luxembourg attributed to Thomas Francine, the Wideville nymphaeum is a quadratic structure with a richly decorated facade, whose Doric columns are bedecked with congealed water configurations of stone; two river gods surround the pedimental cartouche. The vast interior included triple niches for statues and a semicircular basin. Once a nymph poured water from her urn in an ambiance profusely adorned with precious shells and polychrome crystals; the ground was paved with pebbles, and the ceiling fresco represented the Triumph of Apollo.[42]

The format of these nymphaea in the style of antique triumphal arches is related distantly to Serlio's rustic order, to Sambin's terms, and to such contemporary works of architecture and engineering as Inigo Jones's Danby Gate and Alexandre Francini's *Livre d'architecture contenant plusieurs portiques de différentes inventions sur les cinq orders de colonnes . . .* of 1631. Baroque and even grotesque taste is manifest in a portico by Francini, Florentine and engineer to King Louis XIII; its dripping congelations bear a strong resemblance to those grotto-fountains that became so popular in Paris in the late-eighteenth century.[43] Francesco Fanelli's grotto-portal goes far beyond Serlio's examples and even beyond the representations in Sambin's *Oeuvre de la diversité des termes*, published in Lyon in 1572. The figure of Atlas in Fanelli's work is truly ex-

65. Luxembourg Palace, Paris. Nymphaeum, ca. 1620, T. Francini, S. De Brosse. Photo by Atget, ca. 1900.

66. Grotto facade, rustic portal. Etching by F. Fanelli, Paris, ca. 1690.

treme—he appears almost crushed by his insurmountable load as he bends within a stalactitic rustic arch.

A feast of cascades and grottoes is found in Cardinal Richelieu's modest country seat, the Château of Ruel, built in 1638. In his famous diary, John Evelyn describes the *rocaille* grotto "of this paradise. . .the shellwork in the shape of Satyrs, and other wild fancies: in the middle stands a marble table, on which a fountain plays in divers forms of glasses, cups, crosses, fans, crowns and etc. . . ."[44] Divers types of grottoes were designed for Ruel—both the natural and the architectonic.

67. Ruel, château. *Rocaille* grotto, 1638. Etching by I. Silvestre, *Veues du chasteau et du jardin de Ruel,* Paris, 1661.

71

Triumph of Art over Nature

Louis XIV's incorporation of Vaux-le-Vicomte, built for his Minister of Finance, into the grand scheme of Versailles is too well known to bear repetition here. Despite its relative lack of allegory, the decoration proposed to ornament the grotto is ingenious; it is a hybrid work made to please a public with varied tastes. Fragment III of La Fontaine's *Le Songe de Vaux,* "Aventure d'un saumon et d'un estrugeon," introduces the grotto. Two fish, emissaries of Neptune, offer Fouquet such petrified treasures of the Maritime Empire as amber, mother-of-pearl, coral, and marble, with which to embellish the rocks forming the grotto and the cascade. Here the poet intercedes, suggesting aquatic creatures as suitable sculptural accompaniments to the principal ornament — water.[45]

The grotto at Vaux forms a veritable climax to the gardens beyond the canal. Its large, roughly surfaced sandstone staircases lead to a terrace and from there up a gentle slope to the figure of Hercules, which crowns the whole and is visible from all angles of the château and gardens. In some ways, the entity is close to the Versailles Orangerie with its terrace and retaining wall flanked by stairs, its balustrade once decorated with statues, and Vaux's Farnese Hercules hinting at royal power. Seven deeply recessed and vaulted shell-shaped niches are separated by embossed terms. Each niche is bedecked with an artificial rock from which water flows as from a natural cascade. At either end, in grottoes decorated with stalactites, are the river gods of the Tiber and the Argenteuil, supported on urns.[46] Silvestre's engraving of Vaux-le-Vicomte shows eight statues, now gone, and grand sandstone lions with cornucopias. Further on are statues representing the four parts of the earth and Le Nôtre's jetting waters within *ronds d'eaux* at the four angles of the

68. Vaux-le-Vicomte. Grotto, 1656–1661, A. Le Nôtre. Engraving by I. Silvestre, mid-seventeenth century.

magisterial composition. The whole is so splendid that it is not surprising the grand monarch took over.

André Félibien's *Description de la grotte de Versailles*, published in Paris in 1676, conveys some idea of this "palais de rêve...lieu de délices et de surprises." He wrote, "One can say at Versailles that it is a place where Art works alone, and that Nature seems to have abandoned...but there is no other place in all this Royal House where Art has succeeded more happily than in the Grotto of Thetis."[47] And indeed, in this grotto the victory of art could scarcely be more definitive. Responding to an idea of the domain of Thetis, the artists have simulated an edifice for the goddess of the sea. To the poets it is a structure that is so artful it appears to have been built not by the hands of man but by nature herself. That all the accounts make mention of this dichotomy shows the grotto to be truly reflective of Ovid's description of Thetis' cave and its ambiguous position between art and nature: "whether made by nature or by man is hard to tell" (*Met*.2.234-37). Thus the grotto reinforces the idea of an unnatural, unreal atmosphere where all is subject to metamorphosis.

Even amid the multitude of nymphaea in the guise of elaborate water theatres at Versailles, the Grotto of Thetis was the grand luminary of the garden. For it stands at the climax of the astrological myth of the entire complex—the completion of Apollo's solar course and his return to rest in the dwelling of the goddess Thetis.[48] Built between 1664-65 at the north side of the principal château (today the site of the vestibule of the chapel), the grotto was in reality a small casino, an isolated structure with a host of hydraulic diversions within. Rays of the sun emanate from the iron grill, while jets of water rise from the ground before and within the grotto. A reservoir above the terrace supplied the waterworks.[49]

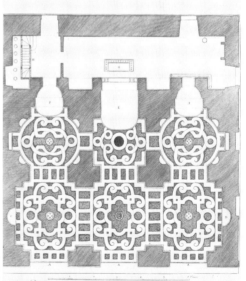

69. Versailles. Grotto of Thetis, 1664–1665. Plan. Etching by J. Le Pautre, from A. Félibien, *Description de la Grotte de Versailles*, Paris, 1676.

70. Versailles. Grotto of Thetis, 1664–1672. Interior. Etching by J. Le Pautre, from A. Félibien, *Description de la Grotte de Versailles*, Paris, 1676.

The triumphal arch scheme on the exterior of the grotto is reflected in the three niches on the interior, while the theme of the facade panels, the descent of Apollo's chariot into the sea at day's end, is consummated within. Here, indeed, is the glory of the grotto: Apollo, at rest, attended by his nymphs, occupies the center stage as lateral wings enclose tableaux of his horses groomed by tritons. The sole purpose of the whole is to render homage to the Sun god, Apollo, and by extension, to the king, Louis. The interior walls were truly dazzling, encrusted with all manner of precious stones, mother-of-pearl, polychromed pebbles, *rocaille*, coral, multicolored petrifications of shells, enamels, mirrors, and glass reflecting the sun, as well as revetments of fleurs-de-lys, dragons, tritons, sirens, and birds. "One might well fancy oneself in the middle of a grove where a thousand birds answer one another." Thus Mlle. de Scudery described the natural music reproduced by the hydraulic organ ordered by Louis in 1666.[50] One thinks back to the grottoes of Pratolino, St. Germain-en-Laye, and Heidelberg.

La Fontaine, at the beginning of his *Amours de Psyché et de Cupidon*, sings the wonders of this marvelous pavilion, praising the "lustre of the rocks and the crystal liquid" that animated the vault. Receiving water from the reservoir above, the jets are depicted as rising and falling to shatter in thousands of sparkling pieces.[51] The complete identification of Louis with Apollo is thus affirmed.

No praises of Versailles were more voluble than those of Mlle. de Scudery, who, in *La Promenade de Versailles*, presents a park that bears little resemblance to the one we encounter in the often cited *Mémoires* of the courtier Saint-Simon. In her words, the multitude of beautiful objects "ravished the eyes," "charmed the ears," and "astonished the spirit" of beholders. She describes

74

such miracles as the jet of enormous prodigiousness, which shot upward with such force that it pierced the height of the grotto and almost seemed to reach the heavens. Scudery also remarks on the apparently endless supply of waters that made the sea itself appear to be the grotto's reservoir and marvels at the small château with its wonderful machine that set these waters into play. Scudery's visitor admires the manner in which the water, after having been raised by large pipes, is carried to the grotto by many small ones. Above all, she is impressed by the economic deployment of the grotto's waters—that is, the same water that produced all these miracles returned peacefully to its source and to its original tranquil and modest state.[52]

Consecrated to Thetis and to Apollo, both as a retreat and a place for banquets and festivities, the grotto played many divergent roles. It was kept secret and closed at times, but at others was open for entertainments, readings, and plays, or illuminated for suppers and theatrical performances.[53] Of course, no matter what its role, the grotto was designed to glorify the king and to propagate his policies. During the festivals of 1674, the third evening concluded with a representation of Molière's *La Malade imaginaire*,[54] with the grotto serving as a backdrop. And in a more frivolous vein, there were the ever-present practical jokes, the hidden sprays that emanated from the ground and from which there was no escape. In La Fontaine's words, "L'eau se croise, se joint, s'écarte, se rencontre...."[55]

Unfortunately, the life of this wondrous grotto was brief indeed. That its ephemeral nature contributed to its early demise is likely, for the fragility of the materials in the cement, *rocailles*, and conduits demanded frequent and difficult reparations.[56] In 1684 its pagan splendors were sacrificed to the construction, in the north wing of the château, of a chapel "worthy of God, whose

71. Versailles. Grotto of Thetis. Molière's *La Malade imaginaire*, 1674. Etching and engraving by J. Le Pautre, from A. Félibien, *Les Divertissements de Versailles . . .*, Paris, 1676.

king Louis XIV is the defender on earth," and worthy, too, of the whole of Versailles.[57] In early designs for the chapel, the demolition of the grotto was not envisioned, as can be seen in the 1681 plan, where the new chapel is attached to the grotto.[58] The wonderful *Bath of Apollo* was moved to the Bosquet des Dômes in 1684. In line with the change in taste under Louis XVI, the rage was for English gardens, such as those designed by Hubert Robert, and thus Apollo and his nymphs were transferred from the palace of Thetis to a new abode. Composed in 1778-81, a cavernous mount interspersed with waterfalls, in the contemporary mode of theatrical ruins, it was disposed to receive the three sculptural groups comprising Apollo's bath.[59]

The present grove constitutes a surprising tableau midst Le Nôtre's garden: columns in the rear seem to be cut into the craggy rock but leafy surrounds dominate, as does the fall of water among the luxuriant vegetation. Here the mysteries of nature, embedded in the obscurity of the enveloping grotto, are juxtaposed with the apogee of classicism represented by Girardon's white marble statues. Could Apollo or the Sun King ask for a more magnificient resting place?

72. Versailles. *Bath of Apollo*, 1778–1781, H. Robert. Painting by H. Robert. Versailles, Museum.

VI. Splendid Improprieties: Pictures in a Landscape

Grottoes in this climate are recesses only to be looked at transiently. When they are regularly composed within of symmetry and architecture, as in Italy, they are only splendid improprieties. The most judiciously, indeed most fortunately placed grotto is that at Stourhead, where the river bursts from the urn of the god, and passes on its course through the cave.
Horace Walpole, *The History of Modern Taste in Gardening,* 1780

Genius of the Place

For the paragon of grottoes, Stourhead, Alexander Pope composed his version of *Huius Nympha Loci*, the famous pseudoclassical quatrain penned in the Renaissance.[1] After Pope, grottoes became standard elements in English eighteenth-century gardens, with the new emphasis on the picturesque.[2] They joined other such garden fabrics as temples, cataracts, bridges, cabinets, hermitages, pyramids, columns, arches, funerary urns, and statues. The elaborate waterworks of the seventeenth century were not repeated; now the wonders of nature were to supersede those of art, at least in theory. The goal was to bring forth the innate, or natural, "genius of the place."

Eighteenth-century enthusiasm for grottoes was part of a deeper romanticism that included not only nostalgia for antiquity but also a passion for Italy. As the Italians had absorbed classical ideals, so the English assimilated into their own landscape the idealized scenery of Italy before turning to the study of nature herself—the English terrain.[3]

"Nature's genuine order" was also to be found in the landscapes of Claude and Rosa; here was the harmony before the Fall. Translated into a penchant for the irregular, this new mode was moralized by the third Earl of Shaftesbury in 1711:

Your *Genius*, the Genius of the Place, and the GREAT GENIUS have at last prevail'd. I shall no longer resist the Passion growing in me for Things of a *natural* kind; where neither *Art*, nor the *Conceit* or *Caprice* of Man has spoil'd their *genuine Order*, by breaking in upon that *primitive State*. Even the rude Rocks, the mossy Caverns, the irregular unwrought *Grotto's* and broken *Falls* of Waters, with all the horrid Graces of the *Wilderness* it-self, as representing NATURE more, will be more engaging and appear with a Magnificence beyond the formal Mockery of Princely Gardens.[4]

73. Wiltshire, Stourhead. Grotto, ca. 1748, nymph attributed to J. Cheere.

Two years later, Pope's *Essay on Gardens* advocated a "return to the simplicity of unadorned nature,"—"He gains all points, who pleasingly confounds/Surprizes, varies, and conceals the Bounds."[5] Addison and Hutcheson echoed Pope's enthusiasm for the natural site, which to a lesser degree became visible in the practices of Vanbrugh, Bridgeman, and Switzer for the English gardens.

The changing order of the universe as conceived by the eighteenth century is reflected in the garden, or theatre, in its transition from presentation of a comprehensible single perspective view to one in which many layers only gradually unfold. We have moved from the garden designed to be enjoyed by the prince at stage center to that which was to be experienced by the observer over time. The idea of process replaced the idea of the completed perfect artifice. A constantly shifting mood was evoked—one of contemplation as well as of awe, of reflection as well as of frivolity. Literary associations were the sine qua non at this time, and therefore, Latin inscriptions were ubiquitous; these evoked nostalgia for antiquity and served as inspiration for new flights of fancy. The grotto within this garden was often but another pleasance, idealized classical scene, pictorial effect, or emblem on the path to total comprehension. It became a symbol of the forces of nature, or a retreat to spur lofty poetic sentiments. But it was not the mere presence of these mock temples, ruins, and grottoes in the garden that was so important. Rather, they added to the picturesque quality of the scene and often lent to it a somber air.[6]

This attraction for unspoiled nature accounts for the popularity of caves among contemporary tourists and for pilgrimages to the caves of the ancient gods in Crete, Boeotia, Athens, and on Parnassus.[7] In the mid-seventeenth century, John Evelyn had noted the aesthetic potential of configurations of

74. Stowe. Grotto. Engraving by T. Medland from J. Seeley, *Stowe*, 1797.

natural rocks and water. Admiring Cliefden, he observes that "The grotts in ye chalky rocks are pretty; 'tis a romantic object and the place altogether answers the most poetical description that can be made of solitude, precipice, prospect...."[8] But Evelyn's more architectural interests are superseded by the more romantic concerns of curious sightseers in later generations. In this regard, the fascination for the English of the West Wycombe caves cannot be denied. These chalk-cut caves, completed about 1752, supposedly served as the meeting place for Sir Francis Dashwood's brotherhood, the Knights of St. Francis of Wycombe, often identified with the Hell-Fire Club, which as the site of the mysteries and mock religious ceremonies of the Monks of Medmenham is better known.[9] Situated under West Wycombe hill and accessible via a Gothic courtyard, these caves were supposedly the locus of wild orgies of Georgian rakes, disguised as Franciscan monks, and their "nun" consorts. Apparently, each grotto and cave bore a message announcing the presence of Venus consonant with the Rabelesian inscription, *Fay ce que voudras* ("Do as thou wilt") above the entry. Latin inscriptions on a par with schoolboy graffiti were carved on a nearby oak tree.[10]

Once the picturesque was established as fact, it was inevitable that its scope be refined. Pevsner divides the mode into two parts: an early more evocative phase epitomized by the gardens of Vanbrugh at Blenheim (1609) and a later more natural phase as witnessed in the works of Capability Brown. Kent, who died in 1748, represents the middle landscape.[11] Stowe, containing the work of all three men, is thus the pre-eminent English eighteenth-century garden.

Pope's verses in his fourth moral essay, "To Richard Boyle, Earl of Burlington," written in 1731, may serve as an introduction to the gardens at Stowe. Of the gardens he wrote,

79

To swell the Terras, or to sink the Grot;
In all, let Nature never be forgot....
Consult the Genius of the Place in all,
That tells the waters or to rise, or fall....
Now breaks or now directs, th' intending Lines;
Paints as you plant, and, as you work designs....
Nature shall join you; Time shall make it grow
A work to wonder at—perhaps a *Stow*.[12]

Few eighteenth-century English landscapes were more celebrated than these four-hundred acres created by Vanbrugh, Gibbs, Bridgeman, and Kent for Lord Cobham's estate in Buckinghamshire. Here at Stowe, begun in 1713, the old was joined to the new; the geometric gardens were mated with the rural mode in much the same manner as in the villas of the ancients.[13]

Known as the Elysian Fields, the gardens themselves provided a sequence of experiences that have been likened to the viewing of Claude's paintings. They were dotted with allegorical temples of friendship and liberty, the Queen's Library, Temples of Ancient Virtue and of Modern Virtue, statues of Apollo and the Muses, columns, monumental obelisks, bridges, and alcoves. Only the rotunda, raised on the garden mount, remained fixed; within its portico was a replica of the Medici Venus, "both garden deity and goddess of love, the changing figure within the unchanging circle."[14] Love is the theme explored in the Temple of Venus, the Cave of Dido, the Temple of Bacchus, and even in St. Augustine's grotto—a memoire of his submission to sexual temptation. One part of the gardens is devoted to the pleasure of retirement (the contemplative life) and the other to the public domain (the active life). Walpole viewed Stowe as "that profusion, that glut enriches and makes it look like a fine landscape of Albano," writing "that even half of the thirty-eight buildings would be too many."[15] These monuments were placed to summon reflections and sentiments about the classical past and thereby to give rise to national pride.[16] They have been deemed "the visual counterpart to a Satire by Pope. Ancient Virtue should be neighbored by Modern (in ruins), and answered across the river by the busts of those Britons who were truly admirable...."[17] The message was always the same: by following the authoritative example set by ancient Rome, Britain could be restored from corruption to her former glory. In Lord Cobham's Elysian Fields designed by Kent the moral-political significance was uppermost.

Of the plethora of architectural monuments embellishing the grounds of Stowe, a number could surely pass for grottoes in addition to that structure specifically designated as such. For example, the "artificial piece of ruins" as described by B. Seeley of a temple covered with evergreens from which statues of fauns, satyrs, and river gods emerge is quite grottolike; there is also a beautiful cascade of three sheets of water falling from a river into a large lake of ten acres below. And Dido's Cave, where the love of Dido and Aeneas was consummated, is replete with its inscription from Virgil's *Aeneid*, "Speluncum Dido dux et Troianus, eandem deveniunt."[18]

The grotto itself, located at the head of the Serpentine River, is flanked by a pavilion on each side; one is ornamented with shells, the other with pebbles and flints broken in pieces. At the entry of a square, cross-vaulted room, we find a basin filled with gold and silver fish. Within, a marble statue of Venus glows with wondrous reflections cast by fragments of looking glass; shells and refecting minerals set in plaster frames surround the mirrors. Strangers admired the place as a romantic retirement, whereas B. Seeley saw the grotto as the residence of the "Genius of the Place," an agreeable retreat inspiring one "with a kind of Enthusiasm."[19] The "picture in the landscape" formed by the grotto at the head of the River Styx is one of the few surviving original tableaux at Stowe not to have suffered from the neglect the great house has fallen into over the last 200 years.

Chiswick's grotto, almost concealed by clinging moss and verdure and difficult to approach, is quite similar to the one at Stowe. Lord Burlington began work on the garden in 1715, probably with the help of Pope, but the grotto most likely dates from the time of his partnership with Kent. Completed only in 1738, the grotto is composed of lavalike stones and is situated at a point where the river once flowed from a cascade in its irregular course.[20] Chiswick also bears marks of the ideal gardens of Pliny's Laurentian and Tuscan villas, as found in Robert Castell's *Villas of the Ancients,* published in 1728 and dedicated to Lord Burlington.

The grotto at Chiswick is now almost unrecognizable, but Kent's work at Pelham has had slightly better fortune. One of the first man-made landscapes in the natural manner, Pelham was the combined work of Vanbrugh, Bridgeman, Kent, and Capability Brown. Of the pleasure pavilions Kent laid out here in the 1730s, only the grotto at the head of the lake remains, where a visitor today may still peer into the recesses "whose fern-fringed chambers sparkle with felspar and mica."[21] The house belonging to the Pelhams at Escher was built in the form of an old cottage in a valley surrounded by the celebrated grounds. Pye described them as "neither park, garden, nor wood, but a lovely mixture of all three . . . . a goodly prospect stands all around."[22] As early as 1727, the garden designer and author, Stephen Switzer proclaimed this garden "the noblest of any in Europe." Today know as Claremont, it is still declared by the National Trust guide to be a microcosm of the *jardin anglais* and is often cited as England's "most original contribution to the culture of northern Europe."[23]

Still, the idea of a grotto in England may strike some as absurd. Disassociating himself from the fashion of the day, Johnson appreciated the irony of such a structure in such a climate. A grotto seemed perverse for an Englishman, who, in Johnson's words, "has more frequent need to solicit than exclude the sun."[24] To a Lincolnshire lady's comment on the satisfaction to be gleaned from the cool grotto in the summer, he replied that a grotto was a fine place "for a toad." Of course, not every Englishman concurred with this sardonic view. Pope, himself, was to turn a dark, unwholesome cavern into a maze of fancy.[25]

The Cave of Pope

In reality Pope's dictum to "Follow Nature" produced a grotto that was most artfully conceived as an accessory to his Muse. Little seems natural about

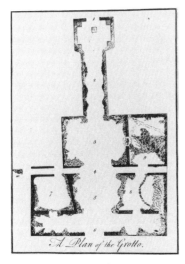

75. Twickenham. Pope's Grotto. Perspective view and plan by J. Searle, 1745.

these walls "finished with shells interspersed with pieces of looking glass in angular forms," the stalactites brought from Wookey Hole "which were shot down for him from the roof of the cave."[26] Despite Pope's strong penchant for natural history, the rusticity of this mineral cabinet was indeed a "labored and artificial" work.[27]

Pope's memory even now hovers over Twickenham. To arrive at the grotto we pass Pope's Grotto Road and Pope's Grotto Hotel before reaching our destination, St. Catherine's Convent, a Victorian structure built as a tea house in 1848. Here on the banks of the Thames, once lined with stately elms and the first English willows, we descend to Pope's grotto, which is essentially a long cryptoporticus. Here we view a room on each side of the gallery: one containing a sombre, virginal nymph, the other a bust of St. James Compostela. Some of the original rock petrifications and shell patterns still survive, but most of the precious stones, luminous minerals, crystal, quartz, amethyst, and reflecting glass have been chipped away. John Searle, Pope's gardener, wrote "A Plan of Mr. Pope's Garden, as it was left at his death: with a plan and perspective view of the Grotto . . . with an account of all the gems, minerals, spars, and ores of which it is composed, and from whom and whence they were sent,"[28] which shows how the garden appeared when in its entirety.

Horace's inscription, "Secretum iter et fallentis semita vitae" ("A secluded journey along the pathway of life unnoticed"), is suggestive of the classical idea of retirement, and of Pope's desire to withdraw from life to the solitude of his musaeum in a setting of rocks and ruins.[29] Pope's letter to Spence talks of his play with optical illusions: "You may distance things by darkening them and by narrowing them towards the end in the same manner as they do in painting."[30] The plan of Pope's garden accompanied by an elaborate description, dated June 2, 1725, is given in a letter to Edward Blount. Here Pope tells how the grotto becomes a luminous room, a *Camera obscura*; on the walls of which the objects of the River, Hills, Woods, and Boats are forming a moving picture in their visible Radiations: And when you have a mind to light it up, it affords you a very different Scene; it is finished with Shells interspersed with Pieces of Looking-glass in angular forms;...when a lamp...is hung in the Middle, a thousand pointed Rays glitter and are reflected over the Place.[31]

This grotto in reality is a subterranean passage that communicated between the lawn sloping to the bank of the Thames and the garden in front of the house, which was on the other side of Hampton Road. Pope's genius was to transform this tunnel, giving it the aspect of a grotto, with its crystal spring "which falls in a perpetual rill that echoes thro' the Cavern day and night."[32]

Just as had the Renaissance poets, Pope adapted and recombined classical elements in his grotto. Walpole's description of it is reminiscent of the antique cryptoporticus: "The passing through the gloom from the grotto to opening day; the retiring and again assembling shades; the dusky groves, the larger lawn. . . ."[33] The effects of ". . . disposing Plates of Looking glass in the obscure Parts of the Roof and Sides of the Cave" must have been dazzling, as is suggested by this contemporary description in the *Newcastle General Magazine*: "Cast your Eyes upward and you half shudder to see Cataracts of Water precipitating over your Head, from impending Stones and Rocks, while salient Spouts rise in rapid Streams at your Feet:..."[34] That Pope was aware of all the metaphysical associations of the cave, of its connections with Plato's cave, Locke's "dark room" of understanding, and Plotinus's notion that the mind gives "radiance out of its own store" (*Enneads* 4.6.3), is apparent in the titles of caves in Pope's own poetry; the Cave of Spleen, Cave of Poetry, and Cave of Truth. Here, grottoes were understood as "the haunt of frugal virtue, philosophy and true wisdom."[35] Affinities have been pointed out between Pope's grotto and the illustration of the grotto of Calypso on the head-piece of Book V in his translation of *The Odyssey*. Like Calypso's cave, Pope's "was brighten'd with a rising blaze: . . ./ Without the grot a various sylvan scene..."[36] But perhaps the last words should be left to Pope's contemporaries; to Johnson, in his *Life of Pope:* "[His] excavation was requisite as an entrance to his garden, and as some men try to be proud of their defects, he extracted an ornament from an inconvenience, and vanity produced a grotto where necessity enforced a passage"; or to Swift, who has heard that Pope has "turned a blunder into a beauty which is a piece of Ars Poetica."[37]

The true meaning of Pope's grotto has only been hinted at. The poet was self-educated, a 4 foot 6 inch hunchback, and a Roman Catholic in Anglican England. Today, Sister Gertrude of St. Catherine's Convent, a knowledgeable guide to this once exotic underworld, may provide the clue in her emphasis on the Crown of Thorns incised in stone on the grotto's ceiling near the river entry and on another stone bearing the five words of Christ above the main passage entry. The prominent location of these emblems seems significant; yet we do not know their date. What we can be sure of is that this grotto is a hermit's cave and a philosopher's den, in short, the domain of the contemplative life. The ideal community Pope envisaged is depicted clearly in his Horatian imitation, the grotto's "TO VIRTUE ONLY AND HER FRIENDS...There, my Retreat the best Companions grace,..."[38]

76. *Pope at Work in Grotto, Twickenham.* Pen and ink and wash drawing by W. Kent or D. Boyle.

77. Richmond. Merlin's Cave, 1735. Design by W. Kent. Interior view. Engraving by J. Vardy, *The Designs of Mr. Inigo Jones and Mr. Wm. Kent,* London, 1744.

As the grotto has provided a mine for scholarly speculation, so it now has been interpreted as a mine or quarry. Drawing on Searle's detailed listing of minerals, a recent study concludes that Pope's improvements to the grotto in 1739-40 were in accord with the precepts put forth in Reverend William Borlase's *Natural History.* That is, the ores within were selected for natural beauty, not rarity. Thus the grotto was in harmony with Borlase's "physico-theological" ideas concerning the variety of nature's work underground as the work of God.[39] Still, we can hardly discount the grotto's function as *musaeum,* particularly in the sense of *domus nympharum,* a source of creative imagination. Cavernous and melancholy imagery permeates the works of the author who contrived the Cave of Spleen.

Pope's grotto was maligned in Lady Wortley Montagu's satire, *The Court of Dullness,* where it was represented as the habitat of the goddess of stupidity and her nymphs. Nevertheless, as Robert Dodsley predicted in the *The Toyshop* in 1743, this Cave of Pope has become a shrine, its treasures pilfered.[40] It is viewed as a monument to Augustan convictions about art; namely, that nature is discovered in (and also brought to) her perfection only by the means of art.[41]

While funds are presently being sought for the restoration of Pope's grotto, the nearby grotto of Queen Caroline in Richmond has not been so lucky and survives only in legend. It was in this royal garden that the Queen built two truly bizarre structures, the Hermitage and Merlin's Cave. The latter was built by William Kent in 1735; its grotesque rocks reinforced by Gothic details, the whole set within a classical framework, was a veritable hybrid, a thatched Gothic cottage-cum-grotto. Within are six wax figures à la Tussaud whose identities are still disputed, though they seem to represent Merlin and his secretary, Queen Elizabeth and her nurse, and the Queen of Henry VII and Minerva.[42] William Mason, in *An Heroic Epistle* to Sir William Chambers, published in London in 1773, attacked his formal gardens in a mocking obituary of Richmond's final destruction by Capability Brown.

Mason clearly delights in Brown's interventions, "which transform'd to lawn what late was Fairy land."[43] Walpole sarcastically noted the "Edifice erected in Richmond garden by Queen Caroline who made great pretentions to Learning and Taste, with not much of the former and none of the latter."[44] A more sympathetic view is provided by Richard West in his poem *Monody on the Death of Queen Caroline,* which records the queen's retreats to the cave:

> Within the Muses' bower
> She oft was wont to lose the vacant hour,
> Or underneath the sapient grot reclin'd,
> Her soul to contemplation she resigned,
> And for a while laid down
> The painful envied burthen of a crown:...[45]

Pope, a visitor to the cave, as evidenced by a reference to it in a Horatian imitation, also mentions the library within with its "small, but choice Collection of Books."[46]

The Ultimate Grotto

> Nymph of the grot, these sacred springs I keep,
> And to the murmur of these waters sleep;
> Ah, spare my slumbers, gently tread the cave.
> And drink in silence, or in silence lave!

The spurious Latin verses, "Huius nympha loci," translated by Pope, warning the "approaching wanderer not to disturb the nymph in her sleep," originally intended for his grotto, is now engraved on the marble basin of the nymph of the River Stour.[47] Modelled after the antique by Rysbrack, the statue reclines on a base "from all sides of which flow a perennial stream into a bath of the most pure and chilling water" and is within a dark alcove with rocky openings providing views across the lake.[48] In 1762 Walpole suggested an equally evocative refrain for the companion river god by Cheere, his right arm upraised, his left upon the urn from whose source the water flows: "This stream, like Time, still hastens from my Urn/ For ever rolling, never to return."[49] A glorious poetic conceit, this melancholy and complex grotto is part of a highly wrought iconographical scheme that has come down to us quite intact from the original builder. Henry Hoare, a banker, planned this country estate on the southwest edge of the Salisbury plain as a place of retirement from his life in town and

78. Wiltshire, Stourhead. Grotto, the River God's Cavern. Drawing by F. M. Piper, 1779. Stockholm, National Museum.

85

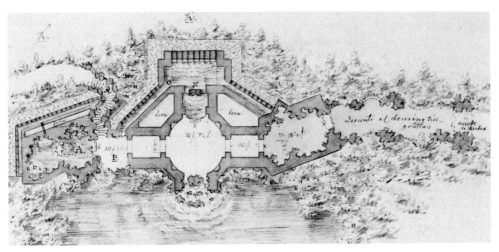

79. Wiltshire, Stourhead. Grotto. Plan. Drawing by F. M. Piper, 1779. Stockholm, National Museum.

named it Stourhead, because it was "abundant in springs." Designed to counterpoint Colen Campbell's Palladian house, the picturesque gardens were begun in the early 1740s and completed in 1748. They were conceived to convey the idea of an endless sequence of pleasances, or emblems. To this end Henry Flitcroft, a protégé of Burlington, designed a series of buildings with "great visual cunning along or above a lake of varied outline: a large grotto, the larger Pantheon, a rustic cottage,..." the Temple of Flora, the Temple of Apollo, a Druid's cell, a Hermitage, and Alfred's Tower. Hoare's aim was the creation of an allegory along a path set forth for the visitor to follow; the goal of the walk was the grotto, wherein the desire was to elicit the spiritual.[50] Richard Colt Hoare, his grandson, describes the path to be followed:

> [We] are conducted by a well-planned approach, to the Grotto . . . in the construction of which nature seems to have been consulted in preference to art; here we see no finery, no shells, no crystals, no variety of fossils collected together, but the native stone, forming natural stalactites, and the *aquae dulces vivoque sedilia saxo,* compose the interior of this cavern; the *sombre* appearance of which is relieved by two figures very appropriately placed . . . .[51]

The route to be followed today is not too different. We pass the Temple of Ceres and circle the lake, going slightly downhill, and approach the grotto. A sign announces that "the grotto is wet but worth a look." Through dark pines and ferns growing darker we pass beneath the archway of moss grown tufa rocks to a shady path rich with expectation, winding branches, and overhung greenery. The pediment of the entry arch once bore the Latin inscription partially cited above: "Within, fresh water and seats in the living rock, the home of the nymphs." Suddenly the foot path changes to brick, then darkness. Within the archway, a long tunnel reveals a glimmer of light beyond — the silhouette of the white marble river god. As we move through the narrow chamber, the sound of water grows louder, and we enter a circular hall with tufa-lined walls and pebbled floor; four arched openings are matched by rustic niches with built-in stone seats. The whole lies beneath a vaulted ocular dome that served as a drain for rain, its sound a soft accompaniment to the source of the nymph. Our gaze is riveted toward a recess at the far end of the grotto, which holds the dramatic yet distant figure of the river god, the source of the Stour. As has been suggested, the image "may have derived from Pliny's description of the source of the Clitumnus where an ancient and venerable temple" stood that contained a statue of the "the river god . . . clothed in his usual robe of state."[52] On one side of the grotto the rustic arched opening on the lake frames the opposite shore, the Chinese Bridge, and Alfred's Tower. But the climax is reserved for the bower of the nymph, she from whom the water flows, in cold, white marble stillness alone against the void.

Through another passageway we reach the river god, a personification of the Stour, his gaze seeming to focus up and down simultaneously, who stands with his right arm raised toward the heavens, the urn from which the waters eternally flow held in his left hand. The way out through moss-grown weeds and porous stones is winding and steep. As the Cumaean Sibyl told Aeneas, "[E]asy is the descent to Avernus: night and day the door of gloomy Dis stands open; but to recall thy step and pass out to the upper air, this is the task, this the toil!" (*Aen.*6.124-29). A rocky arduous path reveals the Pantheon slowly unfolding, but first we reach the thatched "Gothic-cottage." Finally, descending from the Pantheon, we pass through green bowers arcaded like grottoes and rugged cavernous mounts, where the rustle of wind plays like the music of water, to find ourselves at the Temple of Apollo, an imitation of the temple of Baalbek. Like Aeneas arriving on the shore of Latium, we have reached the end of the journey.

John Britton in 1801 vividly recounted his experience at Stourhead: "It will be impossible for me to describe the awful sensations which I experienced on entering its gloomy cells; my fancy was set afloat on the ocean of conjecture, and imagination conjured up thousands of those ideal images that poets have described.... Its seclusion among the woods, contiguity to the waters, subterranean approach, rattling cascades, marble basins and silent statues ... 'Gleaming with imperfect light,' [which] cannot fail of inspiring the solitary wanderer with plaintive musings...."[53]

Graphic documentation of the grotto also exists. Frederick Magnus Piper, a Swedish architect, visited Stourhead in 1799 and left us a series of water colors and drawings of views, as well as sections and details of the grotto chambers.[54] One drawing depicts the plan of a subterranean passage, suggesting the influence of Pope's grotto and showing the similarity between the Stourhead grotto and the one at Painshill. The latter was designed by Joseph Lane, who may have had a hand in building the grotto at Stourhead.

Specialists in craggy grots, Joseph Lane and his son, Josiah, hailed from Tisbury, which is in the vicinity of Stourhead. Their names are allied to the major eighteenth-century grottoes in Wiltshire and in Surrey including the splendid grotto at Painshill (whose patron, Charles Hamilton, had an account at Henry Hoare's bank). The Lanes probably provided Painshill's framework of wood, brick, and masonry and the external casing of jagged tufa, plaster, jutting crystals, and spar.[55] For Piper, the grotto at Painshill was the epitome of the romantic garden. His 1779 visit produced a detailed plan and accompanying text in his illustrated manuscript, the *"Description of the Idea and General Plan of an English Pleasure Park"* (1811-12). Painshill, sited on the edge of a moor above a fertile plain near Cobham in Surrey, was begun in the 1740s. Little wonder that Osvald Sirén sees here eighteenth-century aesthetic ideas combined with the inspiration of Chinese gardens.[56] To the Chinese, too, William Chambers, the chief enthusiast of these gardens, attributed the psychological components of their design — namely, the pleasing, the terrible, the surprising, and the evocation of an "agreeable melancholy and the sense of transitoriness of all natural beauty and human glory."[57]

Built on an island in an artificial lake, the Painshill grotto, now in ruins, is of brick faced with limestone tufa, whose greyish matter is penetrated by large holes that give it the appearance of eroded rocks washed by the surf of the sea. Quarried from several sites in England near Bath and Bristol, the tufa was meant to conjure up visions of great age. And, indeed, the approach to the grotto seemed to reinforce ideas of a classical past. Passing beneath rustic arching bridges (described "as regular as a railway tunnel") that connected the islands, one descended almost to the level of the water until one reached what seemed to be the mouth of a natural cave. The entrance led to an underground passage, winding and mysterious, before arriving at the grotto chamber, whose only light came from apertures in the outer wall giving onto the lake.[58]

Like Piranesi's colossal ruins, grottoes, too, may be a source of the sublime. Both may evoke the sense of infinity as expressed by Burke: "[It] has a tendency to fill the mind with that sort of delightful horror, which is the most genuine effect and truest test of the sublime; . . . that all edifices calculated to produce an idea of the sublime, ought rather to be dark and gloomy; . . . darkness itself . . . is known . . . to have a greater effect on the passions than light; . . . darkness is more productive of sublime ideas than light."[59]

As gardens changed in the course of the eighteenth century, so, too, did grottoes. They evolved from a more ornamental type replete with shells, corals, and crystals to a more natural, bleak, cavernous, savage kind typified by those at Bowood, Bowden Park, Wardour Castle, and Fonthill Abbey. Most of these grottoes are also associated with the Lanes. The cascade at Bowood, enlarged to incorporate a grotto with path and small caves, was supposedly based on Gaspard Poussin's painting of the Tivoli cascade, of course, with variations. Today, the best preserved grotto-cascade is probably that at Rousham in Oxfordshire, which dates from the late 1730s.

Fonthill Abbey boasted among its follies Wyatt's Tower, a hermit's cell for dining located within the hermit's cave, and several battered and stupendous grottoes by the Lanes dated 1794. William Beckford, the eccentric author who commissioned this romantic extravaganza, wrote of one of these that it was "the most delightful spot . . . a terrestial paradise . . . a spacious cave. . . . A place of pleasure, reflection, romance; . . . "[60]

At Oatlands Park near Weybridge, four miles from Painshill, was another grotto attributed to the Lanes. It was begun about 1747 for the ninth Earl of Lincoln.[61] A 1780 engraving shows a lakeside setting marked by a domed, two-storied brick structure, its interior composed of vaulted chambers and

80. Surrey, Oatlands Park. Grotto, 1747.

81. West Sussex, Goodwood. Grotto, begun 1739.

dimly lit passages. Both externally and internally, the brick was hidden by rocks of porous lava intermixed with ammonites, coral, spar, and quartz. Of the three rooms in the lower story of this complex, one featured a cascade and spar-studded stalactites (which were attached to wooden frames fastened to the brick); another a gaming room; and the third, whose walls were shell encrusted, was adorned by a statue of the Medici Venus. Branches of coral, serving as frameworks for crystal mirrors designed to catch the sun, bedecked an upper room lined with shells of every size and shape—the Oatlands Park grotto was a classical dining nymphaeum par excellence. A favorite haunt of the Duchess of York, it was here she supped, played with pets, and worked on needlepoint. In 1815 the Duke of York, who had become owner of the estate in 1790, is recorded to have entertained the victors of Waterloo at a supper in the grotto.[62] But unfortunately, this extraordinary and fantastic oeuvre, built at great cost over twelve years, no longer exists. Cited as a potential danger in 1948 the grotto was blown up by the Ministry of Works soon thereafter.[63] Though dangers stemming from decaying grottoes may be exaggerated, still, the reality of the disintegraton of these fragile fancies—objects of plunder and subject to ruin—is evident enough.

The Sublime and the Beautiful: Variations

Oatlands represents but one elaborate variation on the eighteenth-century grotto, whose form became increasingly refined and specialized as the century progressed. For example, many a garden grotto was constructed for the

89

sole intention of pandering to the whims of dedicated shell collectors. These shells were often from exotic and distant places—the Indies, Jamaica, the Channel Islands—and collectors were very particular as to how their treasures were to be displayed. The *Gentlemen's Magazine* of 1743 celebrates the grotto of Lady Walpole with its shells from the Channel Islands: "Each little isle with generous zeal/ Sends grateful every precious shell/ To make the Walpole grotto fine."[64] Mrs. Delaney, a maker of shell grots, who called herself "a poor solitary grotto nymph" did not approve: "Grotto I will not call it. The regularity is abominable; besides all the coral is painted, mine shall not be made after that model."[65] It was the same Mrs. Delaney who helped the Duchess of Portland with the construction of a cave, in the process of which a thousand snails were done away with. And William Shenstone notes that Lady Fane's expensive shell grotto, "a very beautiful disposition of the finest collection of shells I ever saw," cost three times as much as did her house.[66]

One of the most intricate examples of the shellwork genre must have been the room at Goodwood Park in West Sussex. Beginning in 1739 the Duchess of Richmond and her daughters spent seven years in weaving exquisitely symmetrical shellwork patterns for the decor of the grotto. Externally the structure is rude; within, the glow of shellwork is reinforced by the glitter of mirrored glass. Designed in the standard Georgian mode, the coffered wall surface displayed quatrefoils of orange scallop shells and dusty blue mussels, but the prominent color is shell pink—the vault is pink and white, the general hue of the interior that of opalescent flesh. Here, shells are the construction material of the grotto maker; they are used instead of brick or plaster for architectural details, to define spaces, and as vaulting ribs. At Goodwood, shells are a design medium employed with astonishing restraint and skill, we may even say with mathematical precision.[67]

Another surviving specimen of this grotto-type in an excellent state of preservation can be found near Bristol University. In the heart of Clifton, the grotto is in the garden designed between the years 1737-64 for Thomas Goldney, a merchant with shipping and iron interests. Twenty-seven years in the making, the grotto was praised by all who saw it. Arthur Young, while criticizing its lack of rusticity, was impressed by the profusion of shells, corals, and glittering fossils.[68] Visiting the grotto today, we descend a flight of steps and are confronted by a Gothic facade with cavelike openings on either side. One hall is divided by arcades into three vaulted compartments; seated in a niche above, a river god placidly surveys the scene, while a stream from his urn turns into a roaring cascade in the rocky pool below. The theatrical effect is strong. Abraham Darby, among others, paved the floor with tiles from the Coalbrookdale Iron Company, of which Goldney was a partner. Shells, fossils, ores, and spars were imported from different locales; coral was sent from the Indies; and the crystals came from Bristol. The water supply was pumped from a well; to house the engine working the pump and to provide a view, Goldney built the tower in 1764.

In the same mode is the grotto at St. Giles House near Wimborne, bordering on Wiltshire county, built by the fourth Earl of Shaftesbury, beginning

82. Clifton, Goldney House. Grotto, 1737–1764.

in 1751. Three years later, Dr. Richard Pococke wrote of it: "There is a most beautiful Grotto finished by Mr. Castles of Marybone; — it consists of a winding walk and an anti-room. These are mostly made of Rocksparke: adorn'd with Moss: In the inner room is a great variety of most beautiful shells, petrifications and fine polished pebble. . . ."[69] It is known that Handel frequently visited this magic sanctum, there to drink tea with the mistress of St. Giles House. And what an enchanting sight it must have been: the outer room encrusted with minerals, flints and fossils in a symphony of gray and white, with branches of coral and whale's vertebrae dramatically deployed on the ceiling! The seventh Earl of Shaftesbury (Lord Ashley, 1801-1885) recorded in his *Traditions Book* the origins of the family grotto, writing that it was "constructed by [his] own grandfather to please his first wife Susan. . . . It cost ten thousand pounds but many of the shells although of certain value are of no account."[70]

Not unexpectedly, in a garden-type first created by literary men, the eighteenth-century grotto is above all a poetic conceit and in this guise, all the classical apparatus was maintained. In few places is it as clearly displayed as in the poet Shenstone's Leasowes. Here is the Home of the Muses, the source of inspiration, the showpiece for pleasure. Romantic thrills — the shock of darkness in a natural cave — were provided for the delight and surprise of friends. The grotto was also to serve as a cool summer retreat, a place of retirement for melancholy musing.[71]

That the spirit of antiquity was alive at Leasowes is revealed in James Mason's 1748 engraving after the painting by Thomas Smith and in volume 2 of Robert Dodsley's *A Description of the Leasowes, the Seat of the Late William Shenstone* (1764), in which Dodsley speaks of the Temple of Pan, Virgil's grove, the estate's fountains and cascades, and "a GROTTO of native stone..., roots of trees overhanging it, and the whole shaded over head.... Then turn-

91

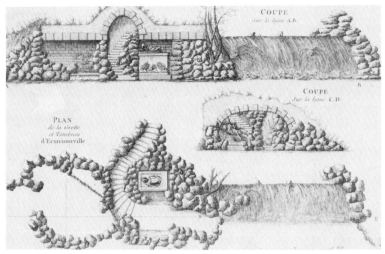

83. Ermenonville. Grotto, 1766–1776. View. Engraving by G. L. Le Rouge, *Nouveaux jardins . . .*, cahier III, Paris, 1785.

84. Ermenonville. Grotto and cascade, 1766–1776. Engraving by J. Mérigot from R. L. Girardin, *Promenade ou itinéraire des jardins d'Ermenonville*, Paris, 1788.

ing to the right we find a stone seat . . . with the inscription, INTUS AQUAE DULCIS, VIVOQUE SEDILIA SAXO; NYMPHARUM DOMUS, which I often heard Mr. Shenstone term the definition of a grotto."[72] By now, we are far removed from the genius of the place, with its emphasis on naturalness and spontaneity. Such inscriptions as that at Leasowes constitute a marked interference with nature, a style we shall see become popular in France as well as abroad. Indeed, Thomas Jefferson based much of his landscape at Monticello on Shenstone's plan of his *ferme ornée*.[73]

France: Return to Nature

By the mid-eighteenth century the natural garden was no longer foreign in a France that had moved far from the precepts of Le Nôtre. René Girardin, the

92

proprietor of Ermenonville, surely knew this charmed world from the works of Watteau, Boucher, Fragonard, and Robert and from Rousseau's *La Nouvelle Héloïse* (1761) and Watelet's *Essai sur les jardins* (1774). In his own treatise, *De la Composition des paysages* (1777), Girardin discusses the means of embellishing country estates and of joining the agreeable to the useful. With regard to the latter, he advises, for example, that in those places most withdrawn and savage, a grotto or hermitage can be pleasant.[74]

From 1766–76, the territory of Ermenonville, which is about 12 kilometers from Senlis, was in Girardin's hands. Imbued with the new English style of irregular gardens, he was among the first to introduce it into France. Resolving to make Ermenonville the true natural garden, Girardin used the materials of nature to compose a series of picturesque tableaux appropriate for the most distant and wild places. Legends were attached to these architectural caprices to induce the visitor to meditate upon antiquity.[75] Foremost among these caprices is the cascade with the Grotto of the Naiads at its base; from a mossladen bank is an agreeable view that was to transport the soul in a sweet and tender melancholy. The manifesto of the nymphs is engraved on a stone in verses that imitate those of Shenstone. Girardin's *Promenade ou itineraire des jardins d'Ermenonville* (1788) describes the path above the river leading to the grotto and the rustic arches providing glimpses of the cascade. Ascending from the grotto via an artificial stairway between shaggy rocks and vaulted passages we arrive at the Temple of Philosophy, which is dedicated to Montaigne; a bit further on is the tomb of Jean-Jacques Rousseau. Designed by Hubert Robert, it was removed to the Pantheon after the Revolution, but the spirit of Rousseau, advocating a return to "natural" laws and "natural" man, remains to inhabit the place.[76]

It is poetic irony that the back to nature movement of the eighteenth century resulted in grottoes so far removed from the natural mode. Still they become metaphors of nature if we consider them as openly in revolt against the formal garden, understood as contrary to nature herself. In Rousseau's *La Nouvelle Héloïse,* Julie tells her visitor that her Elysium is a work of art: "[N]ature has made all but under my direction, and there is nothing there that I have not ordered."[77] To produce the illusion of nature by artificial means was the goal, and the grotto became one of the most popular themes. Indeed, it is a perfect embodiment of the romantic attitude.

Girardin, like Pope, sought the genius of the place. Claude Henri Watelet's passage, "Des Rochers et des grottes," in his *Essai sur les jardins* of 1774 may have served as a partial guide. Wrote Watelet, "It is rare that they [rocks and grottoes] are encountered naturally in places that one decorates. They can however be found there, and by this reason serve as transition of natural objects to artificial objects. . . ." The picturesque, the romantic, the poetic are evoked to obtain *caractère*—that is, to effect more melancholy nuances. As usual, Rousseau provided the initial inspiration, and soon the *jardin anglais* became firmly planted on French soil. Its aesthetic was very much in tune with the romantic settings so prevalent in the works of painters and poets. Depictions of grottoes accentuate the picturesque, both in subject matter and in viewpoint.

Entry to the garden by means of a high stone grotto, comparable to a proscenium arch and pierced to provide a route for passage, is a prominent feature of Le Désert de Retz. Torch-bearing satyrs suggestive of a pagan and primitive nature guard the cavernous opening to this curious domain near the forest of Marly, planned by anglophile, François Racine de Monville, bailiff of the Chambre du Roi.[78] We may recall the initiates brandishing lighted torches along the processional route to the Plutonium in ancient Eleusis, the gates with their inscriptions in ancient tongues in the *Hypnerotomachia Poliphili* before which the hero contemplates his choice, the rustic portals of Serlio, and the grottolike gateways at the entry to country houses. Mérigot's view of 1791 the cave (*antre*) of Chantilly focuses on the approach; we are overwhelmed by the mass of rocks that, when seen from afar, appears as an enormous stone vault framing a stream from which the water seems to spring.[79]

It would be easy to succumb to Sirén's brilliant argument claiming Chinese origins for much of English gardening. French sources to support this hypothesis abound. Few are more impressive than Louis Le Rouge's, *Des Jardins anglo-chinoise à la mode,* published between 1776-87 in twenty-one notebooks. In few collections do we find more splendid grottoes. In his introduction, Le Rouge, geographer to Louis XV, asserts that "everyone knows that English gardens are only an imitation of those of China."[80]

Nevertheless, within the context of the English gardens here examined, the argument for antiquity and above all for Italian origins is more compelling. We should heed the words of Horace Walpole, written in 1771: "The French have of late years adopted our style in gardens, but choosing to be fundamentally obliged to more remote rivals, they deny us half the merit or rather the originality of the invention, by ascribing the discovery to the Chinese, and calling our taste in gardening 'le goût anglo-chinois.' " Hugh Honour, citing this passage, acerbically adds that the French found it "difficult to believe so charming a scene [as the irregular garden with its appeal of the simple pastoral life] was invented by the phlegmatic English."[81]

85. Rambouillet, château. Queen's Dairy (*laiterie*) with grotto, 1783–1788, Thevènin and H. Robert. Drawing of section by C. Percier. Berlin, Kunstbibliothek.

86. Rambouillet, château. Queen's Dairy. Interior. Nymph in grotto, 1783, Thévenin.

In the eighteenth-century mind, the forces of nature were now opposed to the regularity ordered by man. A novel grotto-type appeared in the 1780s in response to this view — the grotto within a dairy. At both Méréville and Rambouillet the arcadian dairy was united with the cave of the nymphs forming the ultimate of counterfeit pavilions. Nothing could be further from nature. The Queen's Dairy *(la Laiterie de la Reine)* at the Château Rambouillet, the result of a collaboration between Thévenin and Hubert Robert in the years 1783-84, is symptomatic of an age on the threshold of a new order. On the one hand, its general austerity—the exterior with its predilection for elementary geometric forms and the interior with its coffered vaults—seems to be a harbinger of neoclassicism. On the other, the rustication, the Rousseauesque imitation of nature, and the hyper-refinement are signs of the waning sentimentality of the times.[82] Set against the sombre cavernous background of the rotunda, the white marble nymph is all the more striking, framed as she is by the rectilinear portal of the white marble sanctuary. Napoleon I enlarged this extraordinary theatre, making it a natural grotto, while a reservoir was added to the rear. This transformation has been judged by modern scholars as symbolic of prevailing taste rather than as an historical precedent.[83] Reliance on past models was replaced in the eighteenth century by a return to original sources, hence, the appeal of the natural landscape and of the picturesque. Recourse to classical literary prototypes provides evidence to link the nymph to a young shepherdess. Seeking the meaning of this odd juxtaposition of a grotto within a dairy, some have looked to Longus' *Daphnis and Chloë* as a possible source of inspiration. Within this work, not only does the Cave of the Nymphs figure prominently, but the shepherds brought their offerings to the large rock that sheltered the source of the fountain. The eighteenth-century attraction for the simple shepherd is undoubtedly a reaction against the gallant rococo pageants. Grottoes not only recall the nymphs' domain but also gardens of the pastoral genre, as well as Virgilian eclogues and their counterpart in the Pléiade and the

95

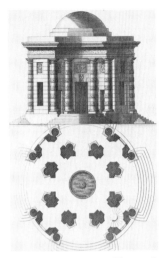

87. Garden grotto. Plan and elevation. Engraving in J. F. de Neufforge, *Recueil élémentaire d'architecture*, Paris, 1757–77.

88. Chatou. Nymphaeum, 1774, G. Soufflot.

age of Theocritus. Thus the Rambouillet *laiterie* in its function as a cave of the nymphs conforms to the accounts of these given by contemporary voyagers to Italy, and by ancient and modern poets. Hirschfeld has dubbed it an arcadian pastoral because of the association with the goat Amalthea nursing Jupiter in the Cave of the Corybantes and Nymphs of Dicté.[84] But most of all, Rambouillet's *laiterie* was inspired by Louis XVI's desire to draw Marie Antoinette to this château for which she had elicited little affection. By the time the temple was completed in 1788, however, the political tides were changing and the queen and her companions had little time to play there.

Already in mid-century, the picturesque coexisted with a mode that at times appeared to be its antithesis — the reduction of architecture to simple geometric forms. This is particularly manifest in the published drawings of Jean-François de Neufforge. Born in Belgium and a student of Jacques-François Blondel, he worked in a seemingly traditional manner and developed a simple pattern in his search for new designs. For example, in one drawing a square is divided into nine small squares. But because he thought in terms of contrasting masses, the results were not conventional. Said he of his own work, "Centric compositions come out eccentric."[85] Among his designs are a series for different sorts of grottoes, such as those in the form of a belvedere appropriate for gardens, bosquets, or parks; many appear to be variations on the *tempietto* theme.

Occasionally architects resorted to earlier established forms, as did Jacques Germaine Soufflot in the nymphaeum he designed in 1771 for the ravishing grotto at Ménars. It is a true souvenir of the Italian villas Soufflot had seen and deserves its epithet of "piccola ma garbata" ("small but pleasing").[86] On the other hand, the nymphaeum at Chatou built by Soufflot in 1774 for Bertin, controller of finances, is on a grand scale and inspired by the ruins of antiquity at Cape Misenum and Herculaneum. A rustic colonnade in the form of a hemicycle surrounds a pool; its eighteen columns are banded with encrusted, polychrome stone alternating with rough stone, while the vault with radiating ribs has been compared to a gigantic inverted shell. Overlooking the Seine, the

96

nymphaeum was probably the site of open-air spectacles in the manner of the ancients. It was designed to evoke the presence of the water nymphs — the daughters of Ocean and Thetis and the Nereids in the cortege of Neptune and the Tritons.[87]

The dawn of a new age, a new spirit, and a new sensibility in the arts are all reflected in the ideal schemes of Boullée and the works of Ledoux. Although the latter extracted from both nature and antiquity a new geometric order, it is perhaps as an expression of the unknown and the mysterious that the theme of the grotto recurs in his works both before and after the Revolution. Rigid geometric forms combine with these congelations of nature whether in his designs for the park of an aristocratic patron or in the factory at Chaux. His use of raw materials combined with smooth ashlar transforms pure geometric shapes into picturesque entities.[88] Little survives, however, of the once sumptuous house Ledoux designed for the Marquis de Montesquieu in the park of Maupertuis about 1780. All that remains is the pyramidal tumulus with its rupestrian mass pierced by a grotto, the entry to the garden, from which a river flows. Descent to this subterranean world is via four Doric columns.[89]

Ledoux's grotto type is similar to that of the Folie St. James built in Paris about 1780 by François-Joseph Belanger and now just outside the Bois de Boulogne. Monsieur de St. James by passing through a tunnel that ran under the rue de Longchamps could reach the far corners of his property. Years later, a Madame Junot, the Duchess of Abrantès, in her *Histoire des Salons de Paris,* recalled memories of happy hours spent in this grotto, of Metternich on his knees before her and their amorous, even rapturous assignations there.[90] Through a grand archway composed of great stone slabs, we see the facade of a Doric temple that in turn reveals the arched entry to the grotto; within is a Roman bath. With its water cascading through the arch of the vault down the front portico to the lake, the aesthetic seems close to that of the House of the Director of Waterworks at Chaux; yet it is far removed in context. We are on the brink of a new order, in which antiquity will create a new formalism; it

89. Paris, La Folie de St. James. Grotto, 1778. Drawing by F. J. Belanger.

97

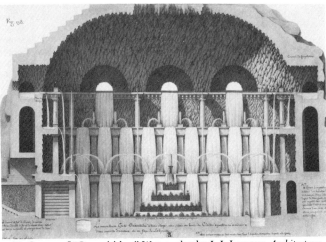

90. Arc-en-Senans, Chaux. Entry portal to saltworks. Detail. 1775–1779, C. N. Ledoux.

91. Grotto of "Oceanitides." Watercolor by J. J. Lequeu, *Architecture civile*, Paris, B. N. Est., 1792.

will become the source for a geometric purism of which nature is a part.[91] The sentiment of the new Republic is at hand.

From 1775-79 Ledoux built his famous saltworks at Arc-en-Senans, situated in the heart of the calcerous and cavernous country of Doubs-Jura. Although sharing none of the characteristics of the garden, the grotto here, as part of Ledoux's ideal city of Chaux, comes once again to serve as a gateway and as a place of passage. One enters the complex through a niche of massive rocks, a cave within a cubic block, before which rises a Doric, hexastyle portico, its entablature now mutilated. In this work the classic is joined to the romantic, the elemental to the refined, the rational to the irrational, the whole resulting in a unique synthesis of nature and the antique.[92] Viewed in terms of a grand tableau, there is an astonishing play of contrast and antithesis and a colossalness of scale embodied in the enormous acretions of rock salt pouring from overturned urns at the entry portal.[93] In his treatise Ledoux, speaking of the view of the entry gate of the saltworks at Chaux, expresses wonder at the effect of his own work: "What are these overturned urns that appear before my eyes? These torrents of water which congeal and stretch their frozen waves to prolong the shadows that the sun displaces for the sake (pleasure) of art? What is this cave cut from the earth to be joined with the celestial vault? . . . The Giants have detached the rock from the summit of the mountains. . . ."[94]

All the properties of a grotto are visible in the House of the Director of Waterworks at Chaux, from which a cascade of water flows through a cylindrical core. Long cited as the perfect embodiment of form following function, the building seems to speak its meaning and its purpose.[95] Here is the symbol of nature in the service of man, the paragon of *architecture parlante*. Thus is *caractère* conveyed: it is concerned with effects, with expression and with poetry.

Ledoux provides a connecting link to the more mystical aspects of the late eighteenth-century grotto, specifically, those relative to it as a place where initiatory rites were performed. In the contemporary lodges of the Free-

98

masons, for example, rites were carried out that appear to parallel those of the West Wycombe caves (both seem to be the descendants of antique Bacchic societies). An account by William Beckford tells of his visit in 1784 to a lodge some distance from Paris in the company of its architect, Ledoux. As a sequence of spaces, the lodge may be compared to the allegorical representation of the landscape of the Elysian fields as depicted in the *jardin anglais*. The architectural layout of the route of the catechumens has been explained by Jean-Jacques Lequeu in his watercolor of a *Subterranean Labyrinth for a Gothic House* where secret rites in accord with ancient Egyptian practices took place; it traces the passage of the water of oblivion to the place of true wisdom, the sanctuary of the initiated.[96] At about the same time, Mozart, a Freemason, was composing *The Magic Flute,* whose librettist, Schinkel, chose a set in the Egyptian mode for the entrance to the palace of the Queen of the Night.[97]

Among Lequeu's drawings and watercolors done for the Commission of Public Works of Paris and collected in a work, *Architecture civile,* in the Bibliothèque Nationale, are a few truly extraordinary grotto designs.[98] For example, in one watercolor, a "marvelous three-storey grotto for water-nymphs," a type explored by Soufflot, is depicted as a structure at the end of a cloister flower bed. A small lake adorned with gilded gondolas is nearby, the whole scene illuminated for divers effects.[99] Elaborate instructions are given for the materials to be used — from brick to stone incrustation to organic putrifying substances — and for construction of the waterworks.

Another figure shows a cross section of a cavern to be created in a small park to simulate the delectable gardens of Isis and the Fortunate Isles — the paradise also known as the Isles of the Blest. Directions are given for the flow of the River Alpheus at the foot of the mountain and for a natural waterfall. The upright mechanism at the summit of the vault in the cupola illuminates the nymph Arethusa, described by Lequeu as "the indifferent Nymph, of a singular beauty [who] sleeps graciously: she is of white alabaster." According to Lequeu's description, women who bathe in the cavern's waters undergo

92. Nymph grotto. Cross-section. Watercolor by J. J. Lequeu, *Architecture civile*, Paris, B. N. Est., 1792.

99

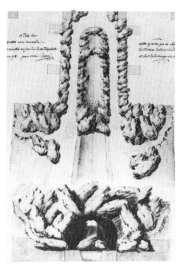

93. Montreuil. Plan of Grotto, 1783.

94. Versailles, Petit Trianon. Grotto, 1780.

purification. A serpentine gallery leads to the most delightful garden where above porpyhry altars in each arcade is a divine nymph. Aromatic herbs and flowers are strewn upon the ground — here, indeed, is an Arcadian dream.

Toward the end of the century, Milton's "umbrageous grots, and caves of cool recess" had almost had their day. In 1760 Dézallier D'Argenville in *La Théorie et la pratique du jardinage* wrote that "perspectives and grottoes are now almost no more à la mode, . . .(one has let fallen in ruin those of Versailles, Meudon, St. Cloud, Ruel. . .those grottoes placed ordinarily at the end of allées and beneath terraces. . .)." And the charming buildings accompanying these were just as readily seen as false pavilions and fake temples. Abbé Delille, in a poem *Les Jardins ou l'art d'embellir les paysages* published in 1782, voiced his disenchantment by calling for an end to this "chaos of architecture."[100] Nevertheless, grottoes continued to appear at this time, nor did flights of fancy diminish. Witness, for example, the grottolike dining room in the winter garden of Parc Monceau built for the Duc de Chartres from 1780 to 1793. Music from the gallery above floated through the crevises of vaulted rock to the complete wonder and delight of the assembled company.[101]

By the 1780s little time for frivolity remained in France, barely enough for a few royal caprices. Near Versailles at Montreuil, a grotto was built in 1783 in the English garden of Madame Elizabeth, sister of Louis XVI. Jean-Jacques Huvé, Inspector of the Royal Buildings at Versailles, describes a small river beginning and ending in the grotto, which was situated on an isle accessible via a bridge.[102] What subliminal intentions are here conveyed by this singular plan?

Just about the same time, Marie Antoinette had a grotto built at the Trianon. The element of surprise dominates the picturesque approach with its sinuous paths, meandering rivulets, and cascade leading to the rock-cut frame of the low entry. Laden with moss and freshened by a stream, the soft ground itself invited repose; the arched openings within yielded views across the flowery meadows, and the whole provided an escape from courtly cares. But the age of innocence had ended: the arches were built to reveal intruders and the hidden stairs led to a lookout point. Unfortunately Marie Antoinette was unable to revel in the delights of her retreat, for by 1789 it was no longer a safe one. The messenger sent to warn the queen that the people were marching on Versailles found her "seated in her grotto surrendering to reflections of grief."[103]

VII. ECLECTIC ABERRATIONS: SWAN SONG

Spirit sublime, you gave me all I once implored . . . . And when felled trees tear other trunks and crush them till the hills resound with hollow thunder, then you lead me to the sheltering cavern. There you reveal myself to me and secret miracles unfold in my breast.

Goethe, *Faust*, I.XVI

Fusion of Other Styles

Prior to the Thirty Years War (1618–48), German garden designers set out to reduplicate the wonders of Italy. The results, however, were usually suffused with details based on northern mannerism as reflected in the inventions in the Strasbourg publications of Wendel Dietterlin. Schemes derived from the formal geometric perspectives of Vredeman de Vries's garden designs were also influential.

Still, Italian artists supplied the manpower for the first phase of seventeenth-century garden art, at least until Versailles was built. Before long German princes in the main cities and in the provinces yielded to a passion for all things French (often via the Imperial Baroque style then prevalent in Vienna).[1]

Largely because of their ability to deceive, the stucco ornaments, (or *rocailles* as they are called in France), indigenous to the rococo style were particularly suitable to grotto decoration. Describing the stucco ornament at Bruchsal and Vierzehnheiligen, Pevsner has noted, "Sometimes they look like shells, sometimes like froth, sometimes like gristle, sometimes like flames." This trompe l'oeil illusionism was part of that Baroque/rococo dichotomy of sombre/light, forceful/delicate and suited to perfection the illusory nature of the grotto.[2]

As in France and earlier in Italy, German gardens revived classical themes through revised versions of generally accepted modes, but records of contemporary individual grottoes reveal no common trend. The grotto in Joseph Furtenbach's small garden was designed about 1638 by its owner, an architect, gentleman, and author, educated in Italy, who tells us that the garden was "so arranged that an ordinary private person can get all the pleasures he desires." Enclosed by arbored walls within a Germanic setting, the grotto as

101

95. Grotesque ornament. Etching by
W. Dietterlin, *Architectura . . . Funff
Seulen*, Nuremberg, 1655.

96. Ulm, garden by J. Furtenbach. Grotto, 1638.

focal point appears to be a souvenir of his Italian sojourn. Behind this small
rustic structure equipped with ingenious devices was a summer house that apparently served as a dining pavilion.[3]

Sources for German grottoes are as eclectic as are the grottoes themselves.
England rather than Italy appears to be the locus of inspiration for Johann de
Walther's grotto in Idstein executed for Count Jean de Nassau Idstein, an ardent amateur of rare plants.[4] This particular view shows the interior of an octagonal tower, bedecked as a grotto, enriched with fountains, shells, and
marine organisms. Views of cities and châteaux, above which soared the
Olympian gods, adorn the cupola. Built in 1566 by the Count of Nassau as a
place of pleasure, the tower was enlarged and decorated in 1652 on the occasion of his marriage; inscriptions throughout sing his praises.

One of the earliest of German garden grottoes, even preceding those of
Heidelberg, is that of Duke William of Bavaria, which was built in the new
part of the Alte Residenz in Munich from 1600-16. Once called the Pretty
Garden, it is now referred to as a grotto court. Grotesquelike figures and
fountains occupy but one side of the claustral enclosure. In the midst of a
craggy configuration rises a Mercury fountain figure, a copy of Cellini's
Perseus and Medusa, surrounded by fish-bearing putti. Statues fill the grotto
walls, while a mosaic of blue stone worked in the Italian manner is set before
it. From the balcony opposite one had a splendid view of the grotto.[5] The total
concept is close to that of the court of the Pitti Palace as depicted in Böckler's
engraving.

The Germans had always found seductive the splendors of the far side of
the Alps. The waterworks of Italy were no exception. As Renaissance
hydraulic marvels had been incorporated into the gardens of Heidelberg, so
Landgraf Carl von Hessen planned the gardens of Wilhelmshöhe (named
after Prince Wilhelm) near Kassel in the Italian manner. In 1701 Charles
summoned the architect Giovanni Francesco Guerneiro from Rome.

97. Idstein. *Interior of an Octagonal Tower in the Form of a Grotto.* Painting by J. de Walther, 1566.

98. Munich, Alte Residenz. Grottocourt, 1600–1616.

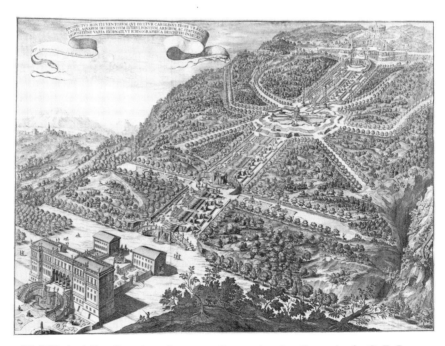

99. Wilhelmshöhe. Cascade and grottoes. Perspective view. Engraving by G. F. Guernerio, 1706.

100. Wilhelmshöhe. Cascade and grottoes. Actual state.

101. Wilhelmshöhe. Octagon and grottoes. Engraving by G. F. Guernerio. 1706.

Together they planned to convert a wooded hill, once a hunting preserve, into a colossal series of terraces, whose main axis would be marked by a series of cascades. Only the upper part was executed, as we see from Guerneiro's perspective view of the whole depicted in a copper engraving of 1706. At the time of Charles's death in 1730, the geometric French planning, so marked in the orthogonal avenues of the park, was accompanied by the rise of the English manner, as evidenced by the winding irregular paths, the rustic glades harboring classical ruins, and monuments rich in literary allusions—Virgil's tomb, Pluto's cave, and Apollo's temple. The formal grandeur of much of the Italian scheme was thus diminished.[6]

But what remains astonishes. Poised on a pyramidal base, a replica of the Farnese Hercules crowns the summit of the hill. Supporting this monument is an octagonal pavilion, seemingly born from the rock, that served as both a summer house and a reservoir for the fountain. The combined height of the monument-cum-pavilion is an impressive 71 meters. The view toward the Hercules is as overwhelming as the view the colossal figure commands, for it looks down upon a terrace where a jet stream rises more than 12 meters high from a giant's mouth. Descending, we reach a terrace marked by the Grotto of Pan, which is adorned with waterworks springing from all sides and drenching any who succumb to the charms of Pan and his entourage. At the Octagon, an enormous water staircase begins its descent over craggy rocks and down 825 steps. Forming a veil over the Grotto of Neptune, the cascade plummets into the great pool at its base before embarking on its downstream course. As originally planned, its long journey would have terminated in an imposing semicircular water theatre at the base of the castle. Instead the cascade pursuing its direct course pours into the Grotto of Neptune, thereby completing only one-third of its destined voyage. Guerneiro's plans for this winter palace were published in *Delineatio Montis* (Rome, 1705; Kassel, 1706).[7] In his dedication to Prince Charles, the Roman architect tries to recreate the magnificence of the original, confessing to be the "mere instru-

104

ment of this vast oeuvre, which originates in the sublime ideas of Charles himself"; drawing from this light Guerneiro gathers "the waters in the corridors and subterranean channels . . . directing their courses to the sea of your Graces, as to their veritable source." To the reader, Guernerio writes of the impossibility of representing "all of this superb building, raised by nature rather than by art on this high mountain." The plates are fantastic, designed so that the "mind may comprehend from afar what the eyes may view from nearby." Here is a feast of grottoes ranging from the Octagon with its travertine walls worked in the form of massive rocks, to grottoes whose vaults and arcades are lined with stones and shells of variegated colors, all set midst cascades, waterfalls, and mock Roman ruins.

Many paths lead to the Hercules and the ascent is neither direct nor simple. Winding trails characterize the landscape, within which the classical monuments that suddenly come into view stir memories of antiquity. As in English romantic gardens, the classical past is evoked at every turn: from the Temple of Apollo, one proceeds to the Roman aqueduct, both of whose views are extraordinarily picturesque. We deviate to subsidiary routes to visit Virgil's Tomb, the Pyramid, and the Grotto of the Sibyl before arriving at Pluto's Grotto, where as in French formal gardens, the principal axis once more comes into sight. Flame-colored glass portals marked the entry to this grotto, in imitation of Pluto's journey through the fire of hell. Niches are occupied by Hercules retrieving Alcestes from the underworld, the three furies and nymphs, and Orpheus and Eurydice. Near the grotto a short ascent leads to the Devil's Bridge. Both philosophical allusions and mythological references are interwoven here to reinforce ideas of antiquity as one wanders through the park. Hercules is the summit of the peregrination and from the base of his lofty eminence, we are drawn back to the domain of the Landgrave and to the city of Kassel beyond.

Introduction to Classicism

Wilhelmshöhe is unique, "One of the most wonderful places in all Europe," as said Sacherverell Stevens of it in 1759.[8] And if Wilhelmshöhe is a marvelous amalgam of Italian, English, and French design enhanced by a propitious site, Schwetzingen, despite its forays into bygone ages, is but an unimposing imitation of Versailles. Here the French fashion as learned from the *Théorie et pratique des jardins* is combined with the groves and serpentine lines of the *jardin anglais*. Just two miles outside of Heidelberg, the gardens were laid out in the formal style from 1753-70. In this summer residence of the Palatinate Electors, Charles Theodore of Bavaria built an enchanted garden as a political symbol of the surrounding world and a nostalgic evocation of an early Roman province. That this dream did not meet with complete approval is apparent in the reaction of the theorist Hirschfeld; in visiting the garden in the years 1784-85, he deplored its bad taste and the attempt to turn it into a picturesque park.[9]

Hirschfeld's disapproval did not prevent others from calling Schwetzingen the most beautiful garden in Germany. Still it is really too big — not sufficiently rigorous for France, nor romantic enough for England. In late summer, early signs of autumn haze emphasize the melancholy of the place and reinforce its quasi-neglected state. The promenade can be frustrating: one reaches the end of a long *allée* or a monumentally scaled lawn only to be met by insurpassible aqueous barriers, whether a fountain, lake, moat, or pond. The plan bespeaks an autocratic power who has dictated the course to be followed but in a playful spirit has added "the unexpected, confusing and labyrinthian"[10] For example, a long trench prevents our approaching the Temple, or Grove of Apollo from the rear, though it is visible from afar. Apollo and his lyre grace the very center of the temple, whose circular form rises from a grotto mound, the Hill of Parnassus. Two reclining water nymphs bear urns of flowing water. Art here literally surmounts nature — the classical temple is set upon the rupestral grotto. The whole scene served as a natural theatre, with the terrace in front acting as the stage.

The Grove of Apollo in the form of a temple is but one of the many allusions to antiquity in the garden. Pan peering from his shady nook is somehow ominous; playing on his pipes, he is not only the god of shepherds but also the Greek satyr, the robber of nymphs and Roman fauns, the god of lust and merriment. Today's guide alludes to him as "the smiling seducer of Schwetzingen park."[11]

Ecclesiastical Gardens: The *Sala Terrena*

While Wilhelmshöhe and Schwetzingen still maintain some measure of their former grandeur, the splendor of most eighteenth-century German grottoes is to be experienced and enjoyed largely in the annals of art. These record the once grand palaces built by princes who were usually church connected. When Lothar Franz von Schönborn, Prince Bishop of Bamberg, became Elector-Archbishop of Mainz in 1695 and honorary Imperial Arch-Chancelor, he came to oversee and occupy several palaces. None did he

102. Schwetzingen. Temple or Grove of Apollo, 1762–ca. 1776.

103. Mainz, La Favorita. View of Grotto with statues and waterfalls. Engraving by S. Kleiner, Augsburg, 1726.

104. Gailbach, castle. Grotto. Engraving by S. Kleiner, Augsburg, 1726.

cherish more than La Favorite, his "little Marly." This lovely edifice, the palace of Mainz, located at the confluence of the Rhine and Main Rivers, was destroyed at the end of the eighteenth century. Waterworks featured a Grotto of Thetis, magnificently sited at the climax of one of the ornamental gardens, a grotto-terrace on the Rhine.[12] But there was also Gaibach Castle near Volbach, inherited from his father, and the Palace of Weissenstein above the village of Pommersfelden, acquired after 1718 and financed privately by Lothar Franz. Unfortunately, we know of these noble buildings and delightful gardens primarily through the engravings of Salomon Kleiner published in 1728, for few exist today.[13]

At Gaibach, Franz's alterations to the private castle date from 1695. Built in the old style, the moat now serves as an ornamental adjunct with its bridge forming a passage to the garden. Details and plan, such as the grotto hill, waters, arbors, pavilions, and parterres hark back to the Renaissance.[14] Kleiner's view of the grotto includes several statues and waterfalls, above which is an open gallery.

Twelve miles from Bamberg, the cultivated meadows bordering on the village of Pommersfelden do not prepare one for the sudden confrontation with the great iron-grilled gates of the Schloss Weissenstein. Upon entering this château designed by Johann Lucas von Hildebrandt, one is overwhelmed by the grandeur of the space. The magnificent stairwell is definitely on a par with that of the Residenz in Würzburg. Just beyond, beneath the impressive marble hall, is the most extraordinary grotto salon, its generous loggialike windows facing the garden. This garden room, or *sala terrena*, is one of the best extant examples of a type common in German palaces. Decorated as a grotto, it forms a perfect transition between the house and the gardens. Partaking of the aspects of both, it provided coolness and shade in the summer and protection from the elements during the rest of the year. Adorned with grotesques, vaulted in stucco, and replete with fountains, the *sala terrena* was an ideal summer retreat. The presence of ample fireplaces at either end testifies to use in less clement weather. In scale and in lavishness the space is resplendent, combining the accoutrements of a grand salon with marble allegories of seasons

107

105. Weissenstein, castle. Grotto, *sala terrena*. Engraving by S. Kleiner, Augsburg, 1726.

and elements. Plaster commedia dell'arte characters, similar to the type that would later populate the pages of Hoffmann's tales set in nearby Bamberg, peer from the rich incrustations of the ceiling where huge crystal-like chandeliers are suspended. The mélange of frosted glass and glistening shellwork, the iridescence and sparkle of quartz and mica, the many-colored gems, and the polychrome stuccoed stalactities — all contribute to the fantasy. Incredible, indeed, must have been the effects as waterworks were generated from the center of the hall, when the garden was once part of the total scheme.[15] Located behind a ceremonial staircase, the grotto room recalls that of Chatsworth. As a garden room, the type is reminiscent of those in Italy, particularly at Tivoli, where the classical triclinium was first revived.

The *sala terrena* is an authentic creation of the German Baroque, derived from both the antique grotto and the free-standing loggia. The rustic, natural brittle matter of the grotto was deemed especially appropriate to Baroque ornamental forms and hence was a vital part of the complete milieu of the château, along with the grand salon, the stairwell, and the music room.[16] While Weissenstein may represent the acme of this art, early examples are the crypt of Salzdahlum Castle in Braunschweig and the grotto room erected within the Zwinger. The latter, situated in the Mathematical-Physical Salon, was designed and built from 1710-14; its rusticated wall displayed statues of Minerva and Apollo and water-spouting heads of sea monsters. Open passages on each side extended the space and allowed for the penetration of daylight. Let the visitor beware, for small fountains hidden in the ground are set free at the slightest provocation, as depicted in Zucchi's engraving.[17] It is in the Zwinger that we find one of the most unusual of all garden pavilions, often considered the paradigm of rococo architecture. A combination orangery and open-air festivity hall, the Zwinger was designed for the Elector Augustus the Strong by Matthäus Daniel Pöppelmann in Dresden between 1711-12.[18] Within the pleasure pavilion, besides places for festivities and a theatre, was a grotto and a nymphaeum with bath, a *Nymphenbad*. Here the memory of antique exedrae and of the Italian cascades at Frascati, Pamphili, and Tivoli was still alive.

From Hermitage to Rococo Retreat

In addition to the princely gardens designed as magnificent showpieces were those gardens in which the ruling class found escape from the ceremonies of court; here they sought solitude, peace, and a quiet enjoyment of nature. Sometimes in pietistic circles, they partook of extremes, embracing the religious and philosophical tenets of the hermits' life as well as its customs.

In the early seventeenth century, Duke William of Bavaria sought respite from his Munich Residenz in the hermitage of his private town palace, which according to Philipp Hainhofer, an Augsburg patrician writing in 1611, contained a grotto where "everything is woven of brass, straw and sticks, and the altar is made of rock...in the winter it is all dark, melancholy, gloomy and even frightening...." Princes and meditating Carthusians on occasion took their meals together in this grotto. This was consonant with William's thinking, especially, in the words of Hainhofer, when attired in "coarse clothing like a monk...although his whole time and inclination were devoted to the art and pride of this world."[19]

Located near Bayreuth, William's hermitage has as its theme the solitude of the anchorite. A building type that had appeared as a *staffage* element, an ornamental structure in Renaissance formal gardens, is here extended to the whole estate. The concept was enlarged until, in the seventeenth century, the hermitage became a distraction, a retreat from the rigors of court life. Its paradigm was Louis XIV's hermitage at Marly.

In the dense fog of early morning, the hermitage breathes the very spirit of romanticism. Entering the garden zone one passes beneath an enormous arch of irregular tufa stone. Built in 1718 the Parnassus of Grottenberg was originally crowned by Pegasus, a spring of water gushing beneath his hooves above statues of Apollo and the Muses. One wanders through bowers and woods, hearing the sound of water everywhere. There are babbling brooks and fountains with classical motifs, a mascaron abutting a tufa wall, and an antique theatre, in reality a simulated ruin in which no performances were given. Within these pictures in a landscape grottoes are ever present; indeed, they were the essence of this bucolic setting from its beginnings in 1666 when Margrave Christian Ernst "laid out this land as a deer park and a grotto house with fountain" was added soon after. Margrave George Wilhelm turned it into a hermitage where the court could play at the simple life.[20]

The Protestant margrave at Bayreuth was under the spell of primitive nature, the pre-romantic preoccupation with solitude, his motto being "I am alone when I seek diversion." All this is reflected in the design of the Old Castle, begun in 1715. The rustic building rises from tufa rocks, the whole seemingly constructed from a single stone mass. Not only is the interior grotto the focal point of the enclosed garden, but it is the center of the entire structure. Its exuberant motifs composed of porous rocks, shellwork, small pebbles, and sirens and dolphins in mother-of-pearl and stucco are in marked contrast to

106. Bayreuth, Hermitage.
New Palace, Upper Grotto,
1731–1758.

the simple adjoining hermits' cells. Here the margrave entertained his guests by pulling the plugs that set the intricate waterworks in play, alternating amusing tricks and such imposing hydraulic feats as causing a golden crown, lit by candles, to rise and hover in mid-air before it fell via the propulsion of a stream of water.[21] A curious toy for praying hermits!

Under the aegis of Margravine Wilhelmine of Bayreuth a new building program was initiated in 1731 that continued until 1758. Among additions to the gardens, the New Castle was built; orginally a menagerie, it was enlarged to form a *Lustschloss*. This so-called Upper Grotto, an orangery recalling the Grand Trianon, consists of three isolated buildings laid out in a hemicycle, once an oval enclosing the grand fountain basin. The centerpiece is the octagonally domed Temple of the Sun dedicated to the cult of Apollo, whose sun chariot crowned the whole; its surrounding colonnade is adorned with busts of Roman emperors in stucco encased in silver-plated tin. The surfaces of the walls and columns of the New Castle, completely restored after being destroyed by fire in 1945, are encrusted with lapis lazuli, red and yellow glass, and rock crystal arranged in mosaic patterns. Rays of sunlight turned the columns into highly reflecting prisms, thereby enhancing the capricious quality, probably inspired by the palaces of crystal and ice featured in the verse dramas of the Margravine Wilhelmine, that characterizes the whole. But the focus of the castle itself is the grand water basin and the tritons, dolphins, and putti who emit powerful jets of water with amazing grace.

From the Upper Grotto one descends to the Lower Grotto, constructed before 1745, where are the most marked allusions to Italian predecessors. An oblong pool, its retaining wall is composed of an artificial grotto structure with a series of arcades and niches forming the backdrop to the fountains' sculptural program. On one side, steps lead to the aviary, an octagonal tufa pavilion; on the other, they run to the volcanic limestone hermitage of Margrave Frederick.

110

107. Bayreuth, Hermitage. Lower Grotto, 1745.

108. Bayreuth, New Palace. Grotto, 1753. Detail.

In 1753 the same margrave built the New Castle in Bayreuth. Passing down a long enfilade of portraits of Countess Wilhelmine and Frederick and through small rooms with delicate floral decor, one arrives at the grotto. But before we actually reach it, we must go from the principal garden room into two grotto-chambers embellished with flowing arabesques and a ceiling painting of the *Sleeping Venus with Swans*. From these we procede into the actual grotto itself, where we are struck by the enormous grotesque mascaron with its extraordinary crowning headgear wrought in shells of various sizes and shapes. The walls are decked with various rock crystals, molten glass, and pieces of quartz, which loom above three graduated fountain basins separated by giant shells. In these distortions of natural forms and in the total configuration, one is reminded of the grotesques of Archimboldo as well as of Renaissance garden ornament. Over the entrance to this iridescent crystal-like cave is Pluto, finger on his lips. What this means can be understood when once we peer into the tiny adjacent chamber: here is disclosed a warm dusky rose velvet settee midst the rustica — it is the *Lustschloss* — and a putto above this chamber warns the intruder to "keep still."[22]

Meanwhile in the mid-1740s, the Margravine Wilhelmine had been occupied in creating Sanspareil, a fantastic garden in the romantic forested and mountainous country just west of Bayreuth. Midst cliffs and caves imbedded in the rocks, she indulged in her francophilia and displayed her general learning by superimposing on this wonderful natural scene others from literature, both past and present. Fénelon's *Adventures of Telemachus*, recently translated into German, is interwoven with stories from *The Odyssey*, such as that telling of the magic isle of Calypso. Here at the foot of the Belvedere rock is Calypso's grotto, a wide natural arch that also served as the mock ruin-theatre — it showed a scene of the escape of Telemachus, son of Ulysses, and his tutor. Within this provocative landscape are the Grottoes of the Sirens, of Vulcan,

111

109. Sanspareil. Grotto of Diane and "Green Table," 1793–1794. Engraving by J. G. Köppel.

110. Sanspareil, castle. Ruins and Grotto-theatre, 1746–1748. Engraving by J. G. Köppel.

and of Diana, all three forming a vast shade of overhanging rock. Artificial ruins are superimposed on raw natural elements to create a series of theatrical tableaux. In few parks is the romantic and literary exaggeration so intense. Though in the Margravine's words, "Nature has entirely arranged the scene,"[23] yet the whole is engulfed by the same air of ruin and distance as is the Hermitage.

Under the inspiration of the Margravine, the grotto becomes a theatre, the theatre a grotto. At Sanspareil a ruin theatre was built that is at the same time a grotto-theatre. Made of rough stones, the artistically constructed stage is designed to represent ancient ruins. The actors performed within the grotto, its walls decorated with blunt stones displaying an overall aura of decaying antiquity. None of the accoutrements of the Baroque theatre with its coulisses is present. Rather than attempting to create the illusion of reality, the natural elements here are meant to convey reflections and moods and an overall atmosphere at one with the romantic landscape garden. The theatre of ruins is not too remote from the nature theatres of Goethe. The drama is in the open landscape; we may almost state that nature itself is on stage.

112

Far more dramatic is the true open-air grotto, with its broad podium upon which plays were performed. The stone theatre hewn in the cleft of rock of Schloss Hellbrun is described by Fisher von Erlach as "a remarkable theatre of rocks, not far from Salzburg, near the Archbishop's pleasure house, called *Hellbrun*; Nature has been the only architect here and has even exceeded what art could have done. Two different natural arches of rock,...form the entrance and contribute to the prospect. Continuity of the view requires likewise no other ornament than what nature has given it, to render it fit and convenient for stage plays, which have been frequently presented upon it. The reverberation of the sound among the rocks is extraordinary."[24] The antique style theatre was cut into the living rock with seats all around; a stage may have been set up for the performance of pastoral plays and operas.

All kinds of grottoes animated the castle and gardens designed at Hellbrun for Marcus Sittich, Bishop of Salzburg, and built from 1613-19. There was a grotto for Neptune, another for rains, a third with mirrors, yet another housing a menagerie, and one with visual water plays, automata, and singing birds. The Orpheus Grotto goes beyond De Caus, adding a German aesthetic to the panoply of Castello and St. Germain-en-Laye. Eurydice, depicted as a dormant nymph, lies at the feet of Orpheus who seems to play his lyre as animals emerge from stalactitic arcades, but the only music is the water streaming from the mouth·of a sculpted goat. Even more incredible are descriptions of the Grotto of the Crown where a jet stream propelled a crown into the air to an orifice in the vaulted dome (a device we may recall, also present in the Old Castle at the Hermitage near Bayreuth). Once the cult of Dionysus was associated with this grotto in the domain of the Austrian archbishop—a reminder of the primacy of classicism even in this Christian sphere.[25]

111. Hellbrun. Rock-theatre, ca. 1721, Fischer von Erlach. Engraving from J. B. Fischer von Erlach, *Entwurff einer historischen Architectur*, Leipzig, 1725.

112. Hellbrun. Grotto of Orpheus. 1613–19.

113

A manifestation of the pervasiveness of the rococo, in fact, of all things French, is present, too, in Frederick the Great's hermitage near Potsdam, Sanssouci. Located opposite his father's Marly Garden, begun in 1744, the Prussian ruler created a pleasure garden, a theatre for the display of riches and power. The king's architect, Knobelsdorff, became Frederick's Le Nôtre, and his plan for the Neptune grotto is part of a nymphaeum in the French manner. Replete with nymphs and tritons and a commanding figure of the sea god, it stands at the climax of one of the small gardens. Designed on the models of the seventeenth-century nymphaea of Luxembourg and Wideville, it is reminiscent of the gilded fountains then being constructed in the Place Stanislaus in Nancy. Handsome waterworks were planned to accompany this grotto, but as with its monumental French precedents, there was not enough water.[26]

Veitshöchheim is the archetypal rococo garden. About four miles from Würzburg, its clipped hedges, hornbeams, and statuary at vistas of arbored *allées* were constantly nurtured by the local prince-bishops. Passing the great sea dominated by Parnassus and the Muses, tripping along labyrinthine paths, we pass eighteenth-century courtiers and suddenly enter intimate enclosures embellished with fountains and ornamental sculpture. At the east end of the park, the grotto-belvededere forms the terminal view. Built between 1772-73 as a summer pavilion, an octagonal casino surmounts a lower grottolike configuration. At first, there were two entries, one from the garden and one from the exterior of the park. As in the Dragon Grotto at the Hermitage, the upper pavilion served as a belvedere from which a fine prospect of the entire park could be enjoyed. An arched stairway of stone combined with fossil-like sponge, clad with pebbles, mica-schist, shells, sharp-molten glass, and snails, forms the open welcoming arms. Odd animals and phantomlike creatures peer from the apertures: an ape, lion, and dragon together with more whimsical monsters emerge from the incrustation of the grotto. The pavilion, once a tearoom-observatory, has a low vaulted cupola, its ceiling painted with a perspectival architectural scene depicting the course of Apollo and his sun chariot.[27] The classical organization is still apparent in the clear, blunt lines of

113. Sanssouci, near Potsdam. Neptune Grotto, begun 1744, Knöbelsdorff. Engraving by J. D. Von Schleuen, ca. 1770.

114. Veitschöchheim. Grotto-belvedere, 1772–1773.

the surface of the Ionic half-columns of the corner and in the antique details, all of which coexist with forms borrowed from the late Italian Renaissance.

We are within an atmosphere heavy-laden with romance, with an almost oppressive sentimentality. In short, we are within the aesthetic domain of the romantic poets. Rousseau's ideas were in a sense accomodated to the German psyche by Goethe. The poet's familiarity with landscape art is evident not only in his writings but in his participation in laying out the garden at Wilhelmsthal and in the design of his own garden.[28] Near his summer garden house, built in Weimar in 1776, is a park on the banks of the Ilum, a creation born of his friendship with Charles Augustus. Composed of an impressive array of garden fabricks, it also includes a sphinx grotto. Designed by a court architect, Klauer, this grotto was built in 1786 on a slope near a water source in accord with the spirit of the times. Thus, it was meant to recall distant times, places, and myths and to evoke a melancholy mood in the observer, a mood reinforced by the dark cypresses and larchwood trees. A picturesque waterfall spans a vitreous arch over its opening and overflows into a tufa basin.[29]

Classical yearnings are indeed subverted in the wildly fantastic grottoes constructed for Ludwig II nearly a century later. The "mad king's" proclivity for building was carried to unparalleled excesses in those dreamlike castles of Herrenchiemsee, Neuschwanstein, and Linderhof.[30] Born in Nymphenburg in 1845, the life of Ludwig was one of perpetual withdrawal from affairs of state, whether to the solitude of the mountains, or to the romance of Wagner's operas. To enhance fully the composer's musical dramas, Ludwig's artists created appropriate settings within which these works might best be played.

No expense on gilt was spared in the castle at Linderhof and the same unbridled extravagance is apparent in the formal park, whose main attractions were the Venus Grotto and the Moorish Pavilion. Planned at first for Neuschwanstein, the grotto folly, composed of cast-iron stalactites and coated with cement, was built from 1876-77 above the palace on the slopes of the hillside as a haven for the king, who cherished seclusion above all. Hoards of

115

115. Weimar, Goethe's Garden House. Sphinx Grotto, 1786. Engraving by M. G. Klauer.

116. Linderhof, castle. Venus Grotto, 1876–1877. Engraving after a drawing by R. Assmus, 1886.

117. Linderhof, castle. Venus Grotto, 1876–1877. Watercolor by H. Breling, 1881.

tourists now wait their turn to enter this magic realm, once designed as a setting for the first act of *Tannhäuser*. Of all artificial grottoes, this one most nearly simulates the experience of exploring large cavernous spaces: from the sharply angled anteroom, we proceed to the enormous realm of the main grotto, 33 feet high, from whence we take the winding stalactite path to the exit, a dolmenlike column that swings to a close with the ease of a papier-mâché prop. Plaster of paris combines with fragments of painted gauze visible here and there to produce this grotto, which is actually situated within a rambling hut above ground. Within the grotto we are stunned by the scene before us: there on a crystal clear lake is a gilded conch shell in the shape of a swan boat. This is set before a grand tableau depicting the *Venusbild* from *Tannhäuser*, the *Hörselberg* scene and Tannhäuser's dalliance with the goddess of love. On the far side is a cascading waterfall; near the platform on the Lorelei rocks is the king's throne, which is designed in the form of a shell. Garlands of roses are hung throughout.

By the snap of a switch one is transported to the scarlet world of *Tannhäuser*; the backdrop reinforces the theatrical ambiance. Another flicker and one joins Ludwig in his beloved magic blue grotto of Capri. Fantastic programs were arranged, wherein mechanical devices used to manipulate the lighting effects created a climax that included a rainbow over the Tannhäuser painting. Like ancient baths, the grotto was heated by means of a hypocaust. At the same time, it boasted the first significant electric-power installations in Bavaria. Behind the scenes, where an electrician and workmen stoked furnaces to maintain an exact 20°C temperature, the view was far from pleasing. But these mechanisms were hardly the concern of the king: "I don't want to know how it works . . . I just want to seen the effects."[31]

Ludwig's creation of a *Gesamtkunstwerk* at Neuschwanstein was based on imaginary theatre designs for Wagnerian operas. The original plan called for a large rock bath rather than the small grotto we see today. Between the king's living room and his study is a corridor that can be transformed into a stalactite grotto by an electrical device; this was partly in imitation of Maximilian's rocky cave on the ground floor of the Lion's Tower of Hohenschwangau.[32] The grotto itself is of the rustic subterranean type with a cascade on one side. The omnipresent swan is etched on a glass door; a chamber within is furnished with two chairs and a Moorish fountain. Here alone, 3,300 feet above sea level on the steep rocks of the Poellet Gorge, Ludwig could gaze through a telescope upon the least spectacular of the castle's views. In this Teutonic knight's fortress, the resulting total work of art combined the illusions of both stage and audience at once—the observer was in the theatre and, as it were, on the stage. Ludwig was that observer who completely succumbed to this dream world. Delusion was the true king in his realm.

Art/Nature Dichotomy

It would be deceiving, however, to end this excursus of German grottoes with Ludwig II, for his sensibility was surely a thing apart. If we consider the grotto as a metaphor for the dichotomy between art and nature, we may turn to Goethe once more, the Goethe who wrote *Die Wahlverwandtschaften (Elective Affinities)*. Here, human nature at its purest is seen within the context of the garden. Goethe, considering the vicissitudes of fortune and the cycles of nature, invokes the "grandfather law." He realizes that Rousseau's natural garden, symbolic of freedom, could revert to the earlier artificial garden with all its restrictions. The confluence of form and content in his novel and in his

118. The Apothecary's Grotto in Goethe, *Hermann und Dorothea*, 1797. Pen and ink drawing by M. Wenzel.

garden is subject to change—this despite Charlotte's conversation with her tutor, in which it is postulated that the golden age is near at hand. "No one nowadays feels comfortable in a garden which is not like open country; nothing must remind us of art and contraint..."; or listen to the English visitor, a connoisseur of landscape gardens, who "could hardly distinguish between the natural and the artificial.... [Everywhere in the park he sought beautiful effects]...a grotto that only needed to be cleared and widened to form an attractive place to sit and rest...." [33] A new era had dawned.

The transition from the profusion of rococo decor to the relative severity of neoclassicism in the late eighteenth century is discussed by Gombrich in a chapter, "Issues of Taste," in his book *The Sense of Order.* Juxtaposing an illustration by Marian Wenzel, *The Apothecary's Grotto,* with its accompanying text from Goethe's *Hermann und Dorothea,* Gombrich shows how much taste had changed. In a passage cited, the apothecary of a provincial German town complains about being deprived of his former pride, a garden pavilion, "a minor version of more famous German Rococo pleasure houses, complete with painted dwarfs, sparkling shell-work and a frescoed parlor with pictures of high life." He goes on:

> But, when coffee I served to my guests in the wonderful grotto
> —Covered with dust it is now and nearly a ruin in my life time—
> Dear, how much they enjoyed the colorful sparkle of shell-work
> Beautifully set out: and even the expert was dazzled By the gleam of the lead
> and by the intricate corals,...True—but who would now but give it a glance,
> yes, I rarely Go there myself, for they want it different now, only "tasteful"
> All must be simple and flush without any carving or gilding—...[34]

VIII. EPILOGUE: THE ARCHITECTURE OF ILLUSION

(From the suttee pyre the flame of gum camphire ascends. The pall of incense smoke screens and disperses. Out of her oak frame a nymph with hair unbound, lightly clad in tea-brown art colours, descends from her grotto and passing under interlacing yews, stands over Bloom.)

James Joyce, *Ulysses*, 532

alypso still detains Ulysses in her cavernous halls, while Chloë, hair down to shoulders, brings Daphnis to the Cave of the Nymphs. Classicism survives in a myriad of guises in a world completely transformed by political and social revolutions. By the mid-nineteenth century, the landscape garden, and the grottoes within it, had become a symbol of a privileged past, of a defunct royal, or worse, bourgeois society. Nature unadorned replaced "nature enhanced by art."[1] Nostalgia was deemed a negative sentiment; yearning for the past, bad taste; attempting to resurrect it, decadent. The present replaced the past and the only viable focus for the art of landscape — and the picturesque — became the public park.[2]

Like many aspects of the arts today, classical allusions are the sphere of the literati, while the grotesque has reached new bounds. Current associative theories may immediately equate the grotto with the womb of Freudian dream interpretation, with fantasies of rebirth in subterranean channels, with the collective unconscious of Jung — where every sheltering cave is a generative organ, the archetype of the maternal and the site of a mystery. It is Jung, in fact, who examined the springs that played such an important role in the cult of Mithras, as they had earlier in the Fountains of Castalia at Delphi: "We can assume that the crypt or baptismal font has the meaning of a place of terror and death and also of rebirth, a place where dark initiations take place."[3] The province of the unconscious, the unknown, and the obscure is also the concern of philosophers and poets. Gaston Bachelard's works explore realms that bear on the grotto, especially his *Poétique de l'espace* and *L'Eau et les rêves.* The analogy of the cave as the foundation of the house, the underground leading to the roots of the soul, is presented in one of his psychoanalytic essays, in which he stresses the relations between the distant past of our unconscious and the forms of subterranean architecture.[4]

Apollo and the Muses, their dwelling on Parnassus, their gift of water as a source of inspiration — these themes form a leitmotif in almost any exploration of the garden grotto. Hence it should not be surprising that the ancient

119

119. *Design for Grotto Entry to Metropolitan Museum of Art, New York.* Engraving after William H. Beard, *Scribner's Magazine*, 1871.

grotto dedicated to the Muses and its Renaissance revival in the grotto-museum have their modern descendants in the long storage tunnels known as grottoes of the Metropolitan Museum of Art in New York. The idea of the grotto is further enhanced by the linkage of these grottoes to the reservoir, once situated at Bryant Park, and the adjoining main building of the New York Public Library. In this connection, the unexecuted designs for an underground approach to a Museum of Art in New York are intriguing. Engravings of William Beard's drawings, published in *Scribner's Journal* in 1871, show views of the Central Park entrance to the museum via an underground tunnel—actually a practical solution to an entry from the park—its arches overhung with vines and shrubbery.[5] Colossal stone figures, personifications of Ignorance and Superstition, stand as sentries at the gateway "barring the avenue of aesthetic culture." The tunnel tortuously makes its way between rough-hewn walls lined with a veritable zoo of antidiluvian stuffed animals to tell of the "rude origin of art."[6] All this is symbolic of the difficulties that must be overcome, the rites of passage that must be undergone, before one arrives at the portals of ART. Stairs wind to a gallery of statues; here, situated beneath a figure of Time sleeping, is a tablet bearing the names of the museum's founders to represent the immortality of fame conferred by gifts to the museum.

Associations between grottoes and the Muses apparently are not fortuitous. The type, above or below ground, or an amalgam of both, survives in the design of many contemporary museums, among them, the Oakland Art Gallery in California and the freestanding pavilion of pre-Columbian art at Dumbarton Oaks in Washington, D.C. Philip Johnson's own art gallery in New Canaan, Connecticut, is surely an extension of this genre; built to provide complete environmental control, part of the architect's rationale for its form is telling: "Besides, I didn't want a building in my backyard."[7] A similar sentiment is echoed by Jörn Utzon in reference to the Silkeborg Museum in

Berlin: "[H]ere the art gallery is buried so that it does not disturb the surroundings." Utzon strove for a cavelike effect lit by skylights above; a downward ramp clad with ceramics that leads to the gallery spaces below was inspired by Buddhist caves in Tatung, west of Peking.[8] And more recently, Malcolm Wells has told us "why I went underground" in his design for a "Museum of the Future" for the American Association of Museums. Solar heating heads a list including earth cover, wildflower landscape, and massive insulation, all of which demonstrate the rising force of the conservation movement.[9] The return to more indigenous ways of building, the renewed appreciation of the vernacular, and the quest for new sources of energy have already driven many architects, engineers, and planners underground. For in the twentieth century, the subterranean world has turned from one of fantasy to one of fact. Tunnels and subways, passages and walks, sewers and shopping arcades, storage spaces and vaults, offices and parking silos and climate-controlled environments have been superimposed on the underground infrastructure of ducts, tubes, and channels. Still, the world of illusion survives in the darkened cinema — which has been likened at times to Plato's cave — and in the minds of builders and dreamers.

Although art and architecture are not without their bizarre, rupestral effects — often carved in concrete as in the works of Gaudí — the grotesque is manifest most of all in the cinematic art. Fritz Lang's lavish cinematography for *Siegfried*, the first part of the *Nibelungen*, surely perpetuates the myth of primitive forces, as the cave-dwelling dwarfs with their hoards of earthly treasures provide evidence of the existence of sub-human lower orders. And in the wild decor of public parks and places, hotels and restaurants the grotesque has achieved new dimensions. One of the most extreme is the Madonna Inn, a motel in Southern California, whose indoor rockeries have gained a certain perverse notoriety, at least among modish architectural buffs.

Taking inspiration from tombs, hypogea, catacombs, Christian crypts and pagan sanctuaries, from ancient cryptoportici, cisterns, and reservoirs, and from the ruins and the labyrinthine structure of underground caves, modern architects have come to underground building as a viable architectural alternative. The technology is extant, its usage long since established for urban utilities, transportation, and the architecture of war.[10] Today the possibilities have become far reaching. Now building underground is seen as a means of protecting the landscape and fighting visual pollution and of preserving the surface environment.[11] In fact, a new science of subterranean construction has developed: *terratecture* deals with building in soil environments, namely with structures built partially of earth or intimately tied to the ground — earth-integrated architecture.[12]

Examples already built range from the extremes of Maymont's elaborate, submarine City under the Seine Project of 1962 to Place Bonaventura, Montreal, and further to the new Forum des Halles in Paris. In the most advanced of subterranean designs, the underground railway systems and the pedestrian functions and infrastructure intersect; the world above is replicated below. This underworld exists alongside that of libraries, schools, museums, theatres, computer centers, and archives, and more recently the single dwelling or office, with roofs covered by native vegetation and greenery. The living land looks toward the sun; the quiet secluded chambers are for meditation and reflection.

The history of underground structures is long and dense. It extends from the troglodyte settlements to the Chinese cave-temples of the seventh and eighth centuries A.D. in Honan province and their dwellings made from loess; from the hermitages and the monastic rock-cut churches of Cappadocia in Anatolia, which provided shelter and protection in a startling landscape of volcanic rocks[13]; to Matmata, the subterranean village in southern Tunisia. All these variations on an underground theme may seem remote from the garden grotto, which most often appeared above ground. But elements of the ancient topos bear rethinking and, in fact, have been recast in effective ways in modern times. Avant-garde architects throughout the twentieth century have been attracted to grotto elements; the twenties especially were witness to the charms of the sheltering cave "in the indefiniteness of its bounds, in the elusiveness of its volume which evades description, in its shapelessness, and in the predominance of the bizarre and whimsical. This fascination derives from its kinship with nature."[14] Artists who sought the plastic frequently were drawn to surfaces recalling the texture of grottoes—the work of Henry Moore and Rudolf Steiner; the cavelike interior of Hans Luckhardt's concert hall, which has been spoken of as a "rhapsody of stalagmites"; Poelzig's Salzburg festival hall; and the "caprices of nature" in the works of Gaudí or Schwitters all come to mind.[15]

Like the ancient Romans—and troglodytes—modern people working and living underground have already begun to adorn their walls with landscapes and seascapes, with forest scenes and animals, with manifestations of nature.[16] A description of a staff room of Manufacturers Hanover at Iron Mountain in Hudson, N.Y., notes that its large picture window looks out onto a grotto lighted in pastel hues. Indeed, the garden grotto has a future.

Among twentieth-century architects, Frederick Kiesler's vision is hardly ordinary, albeit dominated by one common theme summed up in the principal of continuity. By way of Kiesler's Grotto for Meditation, designed in 1964 for New Harmony, Indiana, a Utopian community, we return to Plato's cave. The Grotto for the New Being, the last work he designed before his death, was to be within a park dedicated to the memory of the theologian Paul Tillich. Poet as well as architect and designer, Kiesler left an extensive description of the form of the as yet unbuilt grotto. Embraced by a dolphin bent in a half-circle, the grotto was to be made of reinforced thin-shell concrete; the pool area was

120. *Design for Grotto of Meditation for New Harmony*, Indiana, 1964. Drawing by F. Kiesler.

122

121. *Amphitheatrum Sapientiae Aeternae*. Engraving in H. Khunrath, Hanover, 1602.

122. Architect Emerging from Cave. Woodcut from P. de l'Orme lorme, *Le Premier Tome de l'architecture*, Paris, 1567, book 3, prologue.

planned to be lined in blue mosaic glass. Here, indeed, is an appropriate coda to the architect's life, which was always dominated by the concept of the Endless House, a prototype design with neither beginning nor end but with strict boundaries. Said Kiesler, "its shape and form are determined by inherent life forces." All living areas are unified into a single continuum in the design. The Endless House includes "one's inner world. Communion with oneself. The ritual of meditation." The same animus is behind the grotto. Both are exemplars of the "continuous tension" principle of structure:

> There are two main shells: the sea-shell from the Grotto is surrounded and protected by a large dolphin, the symbol of Christ. By this, I hope to point out our connection not only with human beings, but with the animal world, with vegetation, and with water and fire — the whole cosmic array of infinity.... The water which surrounds the fish, the water which derives from the interior of the cave and flows out and runs around and comes back to its source, should by its sound, give back the memory which we always had in solitude; and in finding ourselves, connect with the universe....[17]

Kiesler's rhetoric is twentieth century, but his ideas connect with the ancients. From Homer to Joyce the grotto has been the locus of mysterious forces, of unanswered questions, of states of being and becoming. A component in the garden, both earthly and divine, it is the far side of paradise and the paradise within, the beginning and the end. A fancy, a capricious toy, it is born of nature and spun by art for delectation and delight; it is elusive and remote and infinite in its potentials. Perhaps like the proscenium of the theatre, the grotto is above all a metaphorical portal, an entrance, a place of passage. To enter is the significant act; for to enter is to acknowledge the distance between outside and inside, between reality and illusion, between nature and art. Like the theatre, the grotto is a gateway to wonder and to knowledge — whether it be those in Colonna's *Hypnerotomachia Poliphili,* the grottoes in the Désert de Retz, or Khunrath's steps leading up to the Dantesque cavern at the summit of the mountain, the Portal to the Amphitheatre of Eternal Wisdom.[18] But like the labyrinth, the story has no end. Like the powers in Empedocles that guide men's souls "we have arrived here in this covered cave."[19] It is only the beginning.

123

Notes

I. INTRODUCTION

1. For definitions of the word "grotto," see the *Oxford English Dictionary* (Oxford, 1970); and *Webster's Third New International Dictionary* (Springfield, Mass., 1961). For the Italian *grotta*, see S. Battaglia, ed., *Grande dizionario della lingua italiana*, 10 vols. (Turin, 1971), 7:75–76; R. Accademia della Crusca, Florence, *Vocabolario degli accademici della Crusca*, 9 vols. (Florence, 1863-1905); P. Portoghesi, *Dizionario enciclopedia di architettura e urbanistica*, 6 vols. (Rome, 1966-69), 3:54-55. For the French *grotte*, see E. Huguet, *Dictionnaire de la langue française du seizième siècle*, 7 vols. (Paris, 1946), 4:659; E. Littré, *Dictionnaire de la langue française*, 4 vols. (Paris, 1876); P. Dupré, *Encyclopédie du bon français dans l'usage contemporain*, vol. 1 (Paris, 1972).
2. For discussions of cryptoportici, see M. Félibien des Avaux, *Les Plans et les descriptions de deux des plus belles maisons de campagne de Pline le Consul...*(Paris, 1699), pp. 35, 76–77, 122–23; R. Castell, *The Villas of the Ancients* (London, 1728). See, too, V. Scamozzi, *L'idea della architettura universale*, 2 vols. (Venice, 1615), 1:328.20, 34, 36, wherein "cripti portici" are allied to "grotti portici."
3. Castell, *Villas of the Ancients*, bk. 2, ep. 17; Epistle from Pliny to Gallus, "Laurentium," pp. 11, 44.
4. P. de l'Orme, *Le Premier Tome de l'architecture* (Paris, 1567), bk. 4, chap. 2, p. 91; A. Blunt, *Philibert de l'Orme* (London, 1958), pp. 46–50, pls. 32–34.
5. Attributed to Florio, *Oxford English Dictionary* (1970), and *Vocabolario degli accademici della Crusca*. For discussions of the word "grotesque," see G. Vasari, *Le vite de' più eccellenti pittori, scultori ed architetti*, 2nd ed. (Florence, 1568), ed. G. Milanesi, 9 vols. (Florence, 1878–81, reprinted 1906), 6:551–53, also 1:170; B. Cellini, *Autobiography of Benvenuto Cellini*, trans. J. A. Symonds (New York, 1960), 1:31; N. Dacos, *La Découverte de la Domus Aurea et la formation des grotesques à la Renaissance* (London, 1969); E. H. Gombrich, *The Sense of Order: A Study in the Psychology of Decorative Art* (Ithaca, N.Y., 1979). Also Vitruvius, *De architectura*, trans. M. H. Morgan, *Ten Books of Architecture* (New York, 1914), 7.5.2 wherein he condemns *grottesca* as allied to "decadent" wall painting.
6. Vasari, *Vite*, 6:551–53; see also 1:170, "The Life of Giovanni da Udine," who sought "the true method of making stucco similar to that used in the ancient grottoes...." Cellini (1:13) disagrees. He notes that such foliage and arabesques are "called grotesques by the ignorant" (rather than "monsters"), having obtained this name "among the moderns through being found in certain subterranean caverns in Rome...."
7. Gombrich, *Sense of Order*, pp. 254–55, 280, fig. 345.
8. N. Miller, "Domain of Illusion: The Grotto in France," in *"Fons Sapientiae": Renaissance Garden Fountains*, ed. E. B. MacDougall (Washington, D.C., 1978), pp. 175–206.
9. Alchemical connections, including the magic contact with the rock, may be found in J. Baltrušaitis, *Quatre Essais sur la légende des formes* (Paris, 1957); and H. S. Redgrove, *Alchemy: Ancient and Modern* (London, 1911). That "darker side" of the grotto is virtually ignored in this study. See, for example, *Filarete's Treatise on Architecture*, trans. J. R. Spencer, 2 vols. (New Haven and London, 1965), 1:246, wherein Virtue is depicted at a mountain summit, while Vice dwells in a dark subterranean grotto.
10. M. B. Hall, *Introduction to the Pneumatics of Hero of Alexandria: A Facsimile of the 1851 Woodcroft Edition* (London and New York, 1971).
11. R. F. Marrett, "Cave Worship," *The Hibbert Journal*, 38, 3 (1940): 296–308.

II. METAPHOR OF THE COSMOS: A CLASSICAL TOPOS

1. Porphyry, *De Antro Nympharum* (Rome, 1518); Porphyry, *L'Antre des nymphes*, trans. J. Trabucco (Paris, 1918).
2. Porphyry, *L'Antre des nymphes*, p. 20.
3. P. Faure, *Fonctions des cavernes crétoises*, Ecoles française d'Athènes, fasc. XIV (Paris, 1964).
4. See P. Faure, "Spéléologie crétoise et humanisme," *Bulletin de l'Association Guillaume Budé*, 4th ser., no. 3 (1958): 27–50, esp. 36–37.
5. See J. Toutain, "L'Antre de Psychro et le Diktaion Antpon," *Revue de l'histoire des religions*, 63–64 (1911): 277–91; also D. G. Hogarth, "The Dictaean Cave," *Annual of the British School of Athens*, 6 (1900): 94–116.
6. G. E. Mylonas, *Eleusis and the Eleusinian Mysteries* (Princeton, N.J., 1961), pp. 146–49.
7. C. Bérard, *Anodoi: Essai sur l'imagerie des passages chtoniens* (Rome, 1974). I am grateful to Professor Ehud Loeb for this reference.
8. J. Travlos, *Pictorial Dictionary of Ancient Athens* (London, 1971). For grottoes in Athens, see pp. 27, 61, 71, 91-94, 127, 204, 323, 381, 417.
9. In Euripides, *Ion* (936-38), Creüsa asks, "The Rocks of Cecrops knowest thou, the Long Cliff named?—the northward facing cave?" to which the old servant responds, "I know. Pan's shrine and altars stand thereby." Also, Aristophanes, *Lysistrata*, (911), implies that Pan's grotto is close to the Clepsydra spring.
10. See R. E. Wycherly, *The Stones of Athens* (Princeton, N.J., 1978), pp. 19, 32-33, 44, 47, 89, 248, 250-52, for references to fountains in Athens. Pausanius 1.14.1 tells of "a spring called Enneacronos embellished as you see it by Peisistratus." Thucydides 2.15 notes the ancient name "Callirhoe," as the fountain was called before the time of the Tyrants.
11. G. Seferis, *Delphi*, trans. P. Sherrard (Munich, 1965). Early grottoes were consecrated to Pan, Apollo, and the nymphs; the Athenian votive relief, inscribed ca. 330 B.C., now in the Stoa of Attalos, seems to bear evidence of this. [See H. A. Thompson and R. E. Wycherly, *The Agora of Athens: The History, Shape and Uses of an Ancient City Center*

(Princeton, N.J., 1972).] In Vari, excavations carried out in 1903 uncovered a grotto to these deities; see C. W. Weller, et al., "The Cave of Vari: Description, Account of Excavations and History," *American Journal of Archaeology*, 7 (1903): 263-319.

12. H. W. Parke, *A History of the Delphic Oracle* (Oxford, 1939), pp. 26-29, notes that early writers do not associate the water of Castalia with prophetic inspiration.

13. *The Odes of Pindar,* trans. J. E. Sandys, Loeb Classical Library (Cambridge, Mass., 1968), *Paean* 6.535; see too, *Pythian* 4.29-41.

14. B. H. Hill, *The Springs: Peirene, Sacred Spring, Glauke* (Princeton, N.J., 1964), Corinth Excavations: The American School of Classical Studies at Athens, vol. 1, no. 6, esp. pp. 1-4. Peirene, the chief spring of "well watered" Corinth, is first mentioned in Pindar's ode celebrating the Olympian victories of Xenophon the Corinthian,*Ol.*13.61, 63-66.

15. A. Pauly, *Real-encyclopädie der classischen Altertumswissenschaft* (Stuttgart, 1937), 34:1518-27. For a detailed study of nymphaea, see N. Neuerburg, *L'architettura delle fontane e dei ninfei nell'Italia antica* (Naples, 1965).

16. Cf. R. T. Günther, *Pausilypon: The Imperial Villa near Naples* (Rome and Oxford, 1913), pp. 51-52, 262, 269.

17. See P. Monceaux, "Nymphae," in C. Daremberg and E. Saglio, *Dictionnaire des antiquités grecques et romains,* 5 vols. (Paris, 1877-1919), vol. IV, pt. 1, pp. 124-32; also, M. Lyttleton, *Baroque Architecture in Classical Antiquity* (London, 1974). See, too, Pliny, *NH.*31.2.20; Plutarch, *Alexander* 7.3.

18. B. Andreas, *The Art of Rome* (New York, 1978), pp. 564-66. Also J. Keil, *Ephesos: Ein Führer durch die Ruinenstätte und ihre Geschichte* (Vienna, 1957), pp. 121-22; the Nymphaeum of Trajan was rebuilt in the late fourth century.

19. P. Bruneau and J. Ducat, *Guide de Delos,* Ecole Français d'Athens (Paris, 1966), pp. 148-49.

20. P. Grimal, *Les Jardins romains à la fin de la République et aux deux premiers siècles de l'Empire* (Paris, 1943), pp. 304-08.

21. B. Tamm, "Auditorium and Palatium: A Study on Assembly Rooms in Roman Palaces During the 1st Century B.C. and the 1st Century A.D.," *Stockholm Studies in Classical Archaeology,* vol. 2 (Stockholm, 1963), pp. 168-79. For scholars opting for nymphaea as grand fountains, see L. Crema, *Enciclopedia classica,* vol. 12, Archeologia (Arte romana), tome 1, *L'architettura romana* (Turin, 1959), pp. 429-33; also G. Lugli, " 'Nymphaea sive musaea,' Osservazioni sopra un gruppo di monumenti repubblicani in Italia in rapporto con l'architettura ellenistica," *Atti del IV Congresso Nazionale di Studi Romani,* 1 (1938-46): 155-68.

22. A. Boëthius, *Etruscan and Early Roman Architecture* (Harmondsworth, 1978), p. 194, notes the transition from modest caves to the grand nymphaea of Imperial times.

23. See Crema, *Enciclopedia classica,* vol. 12, tome 1, pp. 122-23, 429-33, 545-48. See also E. Nash, *Pictorial History of Ancient Rome,* 2 vols. (London, 1961-62), 2:127-29, figs. 842-45.

24. For both the Septizodium and the Acqua Marcia, see Nash, *Pictorial History of Ancient Rome,* 2:302-05, figs. 861, 1064-68, and 1:48-51, figs. 43-46. Also, Crema, *Enciclopedia classica,* vol. 12, tome 1, p. 548; G. Lugli, *I monumenti antichi di Roma e suburbio* (Rome, 1930-40), 2:362-65; and G. T. Grisanti, *I "Trofei di Mario"—Il ninfeo dell'Acqua Giulia sull'Esquilino,* I Monumenti Romani, vol. 7 (Rome, 1977).

25. See G. Lugli, *Roma antica* (Rome, 1946), p. 519.

26. A. Maiuri, *Pompeii* (Rome, 1949), p. 48.

27. E. La Rocca, et al., *Guida archeologica di Pompeii* (Milan, 1976), pp. 285-86. For a discussion of mosaic fountains dating from the last years of Pompeii, see W. Jashemski, *The Gardens of Pompeii* (New York, 1979), pp. 41-43.

28. See C. P. Segal, "Landscape in Ovid's Metamorphosis: A Study in the Transformation of a Literary Symbol," *Hermes* 23 (1969): 20-33.

29. Grimal, *Jardins romains,* p. 306. Cf. Vitruvius, *De architectura* 5.6.8. See, too, G. Roux, "Le Val des muses et les musées chez les auteurs anciens," *Bulletin de Correspondance hellénique,* 77 (1954): 22-28. For the Boscoreale fresco, see P. W. Lehmann, *Roman Wall Paintings from Boscoreale in the Metropolitan Museum of Art* (Cambridge, Mass., 1953), pp. 114-16.

30. Grimal, *Jardins romains,* pp. 306-07.

31. Tamm, "Auditorium and Palatium," pp. 177-78.

32. R. Ginouvès, *Laodicée du Lycos: Le Nymphée* (Campagnes, 1961-63; Quebec and Paris, 1969), pp. 162-66.

33. Ginouvès, *Laodicée du Lycos,* pp. 164-65.

34. C. Norberg-Schulz, "Genius Loci of Rome," *Architectural Design,* 49, 3-4 (1979): 50-55.

35. Ibid.

36. G. B. Piranesi, *Di due spelonche ornate dagli antichiti alla riva del lago Albano* (Rome, 1764).

37. K. Baedecker, *Southern Italy and Sicily* (Leipzig and London, 1900), p. 368.

38. R. T. Günther, *The Submerged Greek and Roman Foreshore near Naples: Contributions to the Study of Earth Movements in the Bay of Naples* (Oxford and Rome, 1903); Günther, *Pausilypon,* pp. 16-17, 21-26, *passim.* See, too, V. Scamozzi, *L'idea della architettura universale,* 2 vols. (Venice, 1615), 1:328, 361-62.

39. P. Panvini, *Alle antichità e curiosità naturali di Pozzuoli, Cuma, Baia e Miseno* (Naples, 1818); and P. A. Paoli, *Antichità di Pozzuoli: Putolanae antiquitates* (Naples, 1768), pls. vi, vii.

40. A. F. Stewart, "To Entertain an Emperor: Sperlonga, Laokoon and Tiberius at the Dinner Table," *Journal of Roman Studies,* 67 (1977): 76-90. Also, G. Jacopi, *L'antro di Tiberio a Sperlonga* (Rome, 1963). For other grotto-nymphaea, see A. G. McKay, *Houses, Villas and Palaces in the Roman World* (Ithaca, N.Y., 1975), chap. 5, esp. pp. 126-33.

41. Boëthius, *Estrucan and Early Roman Architecture,* p. 194.

42. F. Rakob, "Ein Grottentriklinium in Pompeii," *Mitteilungen des Deutschen Archëologischen Instituts: Römische*

Abteilung, 71 (1964): 182-94, fig. 9; H. Eschebach, "Die Gebrauchswasserversorgung des antiken Pompeii," *Antike Welt,* 10 (1979): 3-24, esp. 19.

43. Neuerburg, *Architettura delle fontane e dei ninfei,* pp. 156-57; S. Aurigemma, *Villa Adriana* (Rome, 1961), p. 80. See, too, M. E. Blake, *Ancient Roman Construction in Italy from the Prehistoric Period to Augustus* (Washington, D.C., 1947), pp. 62, 238.

44. Neuerburg, *Architettura delle fontane e dei ninfei,* pp. 240-41.

45. M. E. Blake, *Roman Construction in Italy from Nerva through the Antonines* (Philadelphia, 1973), pp. 250-51.

46. D. R. Dudley, *Urbs Roma* (London, 1967), pp. 220-21.

47.. Love is often the theme, as in Horace's anti-love poem (*Ode* 1.5) in which the grotto serves as a mise-en-scène for romantic trysts. Just as commonplace is the grotto's association with such powers of earth and darkness as those cited in Ovid, who, for example, wrote of the fearful caverns of Invidia (*Met.* 2.760-82).

48. G. Luck, "The Cave and the Source (on the Imagery of Propertius 3.1.1-6)," *Classical Quarterly,* n.s. 7 (1957): 175-79.

III. BIBLICAL SOURCES AND CHRISTIAN MYSTERIES

1. W. A. Smith, *The Historical Geography of the Holy Land* (New York, 1908), pp. 54-55. C. Wilson, *Picturesque Palestine, Sinai and Egypt,* 2 vols. (New York, 1881), pp. 60-62.

2. Z. Vilnay, *The Holy Land in Old Prints and Maps* (Jerusalem, 1967), p. 207, figs. 413, 414.

3. Wilson, *Picturesque Palestine,* pp. 84, 96-97. See J. Wilkinson, *Jerusalem Pilgrims Before the Crusades* (Jerusalem, 1977), p. 161B; Jeremiah's pit *(lacus),* perhaps one of numerous cisterns near the southwest corner of the Temple area. Also, F. de Saulcy, *Jérusalem* (Paris, 1882), pp. 174-75.

4. Smith, *Historical Geography,* pp. 305-06. F. Vigouroux, *Dictionnaire de la Bible* (Paris, 1899), 2:450-56, under "Césarée de Philippe."

5. P. Saintyves, pseud.(E. Nourry), *Les Grottes, dans les cultes magico-religieux et la symbolique primitive* (Paris, 1918), pp. 63-67, 106-08.

6. E. Mandowsky and C. Mitchell, *Pirro Ligorio's Roman Antiquities* (London, 1963), pp. 59-60. Also Saintyves, *Grottes,* bk. 2, chap. 1.

7. Saintyves, *Grottes,* chaps. 3, 4, pp. 166-251.

8. Ibid., pp. 205-06; Porphyry, *L'Antre des nymphes,* trans. J. Trabucco (Paris, 1918), pp. 29-30, 32.

9. M. Jean Doubdan, *Le Voyage de la Terre-Sainte* (Paris, 1666), p. 514; see also Saintyves, *Grottes,* chap. 3, pp. 166-207.

10. H. Vincent and F. M. Abel, *Jérusalem nouvelle,* 2 vols. (Paris, 1914-22), 2:379-82.

11. Cited in Wilkinson, *Jerusalem Pilgrims Before the Crusades,* p. 35.

12. Vincent and Abel, *Jérusalem nouvelle,* 2:317-19, 328, 336-37.

13. Ibid., 2:379-82; Wilkinson, *Jerusalem Pilgrims Before the Crusades,* pp. 166a, 166b.

14. For the discovery of the Most Holy Sepulchre and the subsequent erection of a church and structure over it, see Eusebius, *The Life of Constantine,* ed. P. Schaff and H. Wace, *The Nicene and Post-Nicene Fathers of the Christian Church* (New York, 1890), sections 28-39, pp. 527-30. The translation cited here is from C. Couäson, *The Church of the Holy Sepulchre in Jerusalem,* trans. J. P. B. and C. Ross (London, 1974), pp. 14-15.

15. Wilson, *Picturesque Palestine,* pp. 60-62.

16. A. Chastel, *L'Art et humanisme à Florence au temps de Laurent le Magnifique* (Paris, 1959), pp. 435-40. E. Panofsky, *Early Netherlandish Painting* (Cambridge, Mass., 1953), p. 46, notes that the Cave of the Nativity and the Cave of the Entombment were Eastern motifs that became standard in Byzantine art; they were sanctioned in Western writing by St. Bridget of Sweden, who wrote in *Revelationes,* 7:21, 1360-70, "Qui cum intrassent *speluncam."*

IV. HUMANIST CONCEITS: RENAISSANCE GARDENS

1. See L. B. Alberti, *De re aedificatoria,* ed. G. Orlandi, 2 vols. (Milan, 1966), 2:804-05; Ovid, *Met.* 3.159; Ovid, *Fasti.* 2.315.

2. E. Battisti, *L'antirinascimento* (Milan, 1962), pp. 29-30.

3. The most comprehensive account of grotto types is still B. Wiles, *The Fountains of the Florentine Sculptors and Their Followers* (Cambridge, Mass., 1933). On page 42, Wiles describes an early example of the formal grotto attributed to Giuliano da Sangallo; it is in the Medicean Villa of Poggio a Caiano. For ancient parallels, see especially, G. W. Elderkin, "The Natural and the Artificial Grotto," *Hesperia,* vol. 10, no. 2 (1941): 125-37. For the emergence of Poliphilus from the dark cavern, his initiation, and his metaphorical journey to the garden of Venus, see T. Comito, *The Idea of the Garden in the Renaissance* (New Brunswick, N.J., 1978), pp. 164-66.

4. See L. Heydenreich and W. Lotz, *Architecture in Italy: 1400-1600* (Harmondsworth, 1974), pp. 324-25, where the grotto itself is viewed as the birth cave of the Venus Anadyomene, thereby creating "the counterpart of the courtly ceremony in the neighboring palazzo, a union of nature and art which seems to come from an older, more primitive world."

5. A. Maiuri, *Ercolano* (Rome, 1932), pp. 35-36, fig. 35.

6. D. Heikamp, "The 'Grotta Grande' in the Boboli Gardens, Florence," *The Connoisseur,* vol. 199, no. 299 (1978): 38-43; idem, "L'Architecture de la métamorphose," *L'Oeil,* 14 (1964): 2-9; and G. Cambiagi, *Descrizione dell'imperiale giardino di Boboli* (Florence, 1757), pp. 19-22.

7. Heikamp, "Grotta Grande," p. 42. F. Bocchi, *Le bellezze della città di Firenze* (Florence, 1591), pp.

132-39, pours lavish praise upon the stupifying artifice of the grotto.

8. M. de Montaigne, *Journal d'un voyage en Italie... 1580-1581* (Paris, 1906), pp. 194-96. That these "curiously wrought" marble zoomorphs — "elephants, camels, sheepe, harts, wolves"— dominated the mise-en-scène is corroborated by Fynes Moryson in his 1594 account, *Itinerary* (Glasgow, 1907), pp. 1, 331.

9. G. Vasari, *Le vite de'più eccellenti pittori, scultori ed architetti,* 2nd ed. (Florence, 1568), ed. G. Milanesi, 9 vols. (Florence, 1878-81, reprinted 1906), vol. 6, chap. 5, pp. 141-43, "Introduzione dell' architettura," describes in detail the armature of the artificial stalactites, the distribution of conduits within, with their punctured holes providing "jets through which the water rains down among the incrustations...."

10. Ibid. See "The Life of Tribolo," 6:76-85.

11. L. Châtelet-Lange, "The Grotto of the Unicorn and the Garden of the Villa di Castello," *Art Bulletin,* 50 (1968): 51-59; also D. Heikamp, "La Villa di Castello," *L'Oeil,* 151 (1967): 56-65.

12. D. Coffin, *The Villa in the Life of Renaissance Rome* (Princeton, N.J., 1979), pp. 294, 302-05.

13. C. Tolomei, *Delle lettere (...) libri sette* (Venice, 1554), pp. 41r-43r. See original text of this letter in E. B. MacDougall, "Introduction," in *"Fons Sapientiae": Renaissance Garden Fountains,* ed. E. B. MacDougall (Washington, D.C., 1978), pp. 1-14, esp. pp. 11-14, Appendix; also idem, *"L'Ingegnoso Artifizio:* Sixteenth-Century Garden Fountains in Rome," *"Fons Sapientiae,"* pp. 85-113. Also idem, *"Ars Hortulorum,* Sixteenth-century Garden Iconography and Literary Theory in Italy," in *The Italian Garden,* ed. D. R. Coffin (Washington, D.C., 1972), pp. 37-60, esp. p. 52, regarding the "paradox of art created from nature itself."

14. Ammannati letter of 1555, cited in T. Falk, "Studien zur Topographie und Geschichte der Villa Giulia in Rom," *Römisches Jahrbuch für Kunstgeschichte,* 13 (1971): 171-73.

15. Coffin, *Villa in Renaissance Rome,* pp. 156-57; Heydenreich and Lotz, *Architecture in Italy,* p. 270.

16. Frontinus, *De aquaeductu urbis Romae,* trans. C. E. Bennett, Loeb Classical Library (London, 1925), 1.10. Coffin, *Villa in Renaissance Rome,* p. 156.

17. See, for example, the 1559 account of Jean-Jacques Boissard in C. Davis, "The Villa Giulia and the 'Fontana della Vergine,'" *Psicon,* vol. 4, nos. 8-9, (1977): 132-41.

18. H. Burns, *Andrea Palladio, 1508-1580: The Portico and the Farmyard* (London, 1975), pp. 195-196; Falk, "Studien der Villa Giulia," p. 235; G. Zorzi, *Le Ville ed i teatri di Andrea Palladio* (Vicenza, 1968), p. 178; L. Puppi, *Andrea Palladio* (Boston, 1973), p. 318, figs. 151-53. See, too, C. H. Smyth, "Sunken Courts of the Villa Giulia and the Villa Imperiale," in *Essays in Memory of Karl Lehmann,* ed. L. F. Sandler (New York, 1964), (Marsyas: Studies in the History of Art Supplement, 1), pp. 304-13, for a precedent for the sunken court in the Villa Imperiale near Pesaro.

19. That grottoes usually reflect both the rustic and the architectural modes is consonant with the spirit of mannerism. In the Grotta del Ninfeo, 1570-80, at the Villa del Vescovo (now Pecci-Blunt) in Marlia, just outside the town of Lucca, the two modes are clearly distinguished though juxtaposed. G. Saminiati [cited in I. B. Barsali, *Le ville Lucchesi* (Rome, 1964), p. 212, pls. 19, 20; and idem, *Catalogo della mostra delle Villa Lucchesi dal '500* (Lucca, 1975)] notes the duality of the scheme: "It will be necessary besides for the pretense of the principal grotto to make fragments of grottoes dripping of stone, niches of shells, snails, marine oysters which... present a frightful spectacle." It is the eternal Apollonian/Dionysian conflict—the delights of otium banished by sheer orneriness.

20. Coffin, *Villa in Renaissance Rome,* p. 9.

21. G. Fracassetti, ed., *Lettere di Francesco Petrarca delle cose familiari,* 5 vols. (Florence, 1865), vol. 3, bk. 13, letter 8, pp. 258-62.

22. E. MacDougall, "The Sleeping Nymph: Origins of a Humanist Fountain Type," *Art Bulletin,* 57 (1975): 357-65; H. Brummer, *The Statue Court in the Vatican Belvedere,* Stockholm Studies in the History of Art, no. 20 (Stockholm, 1970).

23. G. Smith, *The Casino of Pius IV* (Princeton, N.J., 1977), pp. 48-56.

24. Coffin, *Villa in Renaissance Rome,* pp. 86-87. See J. Ackerman, "The Belvedere as a Classical Villa," *Journal of the Warburg and Courtauld Institutes,* 14 (1951): 70-91, who stresses parallels with antiquity in his comparison with Bramante's Cortile S. Damasco facade to that of the Septizodium, which was still standing in the early sixteenth century.

25. H. Hibbard, *Carlo Maderno* (University Park, Pa., 1971, pp. 199-200.

26. Battisti, *L'antirinascimento,* p. 31. David Coffin has noted (in a letter of December 17, 1979) that the development of the physical form of the grotto in the Renaissance was probably influenced by the so-called Grotto of Egeria in the Vigna Caffarelli outside Rome. To support this hypothesis, he cites the Uffizi drawings of its plan attributed to Antonio da Sangallo II and Sallustio Peruzzi. See, too, G. Masson, *Italian Gardens* (London, 1961), pp. 128-29.

27. A. Bruschi, *Bramante architetto* (Bari, 1969), pp. 1048-51; Coffin, *Villa in Renaissance Rome,* pp. 243-45; C. L. Frommel, *Der Römische Palastbau der Hochrenaissance,* 3 vols. (Tubingen, 1973), 1:30-34, *passim.*

28. Cf. Nero's artificial lake described in Tacitus, *Annals* 14.220. P. Giovio, *Le vite di Leon Decimo...* (Florence, 1551), pp. 377-78 (cited in Bruschi, *Bramante,* p. 1051), confirms the idea of a country pavilion for summer festivities. Its function for repose is made more manifest in its similarity to Agostino Chigi's dining loggia, with its subterranean grotto fed by Tiber water—a place for bathing and for poetry, a

Platonic antrum—in the Villa Farnesina, built in 1510-11. See C. L. Frommel, *Die Farnesina und Peruzzis architektonishes Frühwerke* (Berlin, 1961), pp. 42-43.

29. See Vasari, *Vite*, 6:556. An antique precedent of the Villa Madama nymphaeum is explored by N. Neuerburg ("Raphael at Tivoli and the Villa Madama," in *Essays in Memory of Karl Lehmann*, pp. 227-31), who writes that Raphael was party to an archaeological excursion to Tivoli with Pietro Bembo, Navagero, and Castiglione.

30. J. Shearman, *Mannerism* (Harmondsworth, 1967), pp. 125-33, eps. p. 126.

31. S. Serlio, *Regole generali di architettura sopra le cinque maniere degli edifici* (Venice, 1537), fol. 133v, discusses the juxtaposition of art and nature in the use of rustic masonry together with the classical order. See F. Hartt, *Giulio Romano*, 2 vols. (New Haven, Conn., 1958).

32. C. M. Brown, "The Grotta of Isabella d'Este," *Gazette des Beaux-Arts*, ser. 6, vol. 89 (1977): 155-71; see E. Verheyen, *The Palazzo del Te in Mantua* (Baltimore, Md., 1977), pp. 33-35, 129-32.

33. Montaigne, *Journal*, pp. 269-72.

34. D. Coffin, *Villa d'Este at Tivoli* (Princeton, N.J., 1960), Appendix. See the entries for Tivoli, Rome, dated May 7, 1645, in John Evelyn, *Diary*, ed. E. S. De Beer, 6 vols. (Oxford, 1955), 2: 396-97.

35. Coffin, *Villa d'Este*, pp. 37-38, 119-20.

36. V. Scamozzi, *L'idea della architettura universale*, 2 vols. (Venice, 1615), 1: 343-44. O. Rabasco, *Il Convito* (Florence, 1615), p. 59; cited in Coffin, *Villa in Renaissance Rome*, p. 361.

37. Coffin, *Villa in Renaissance Rome*, pp. 354-61, including iconographical program. Also C. Lazzaro-Bruno, "The Villa Lante at Bagnaia" (Ph.D. diss., Princeton University, 1974, 2 vols.).

38. C Monbeig-Goguel, *Inventaire général des dessins italiens* (Paris, 1972), n. 368, pp. 223-24.

39. B. S. Sgrilli, *Descrizione della Regia Villa, fontane, e fabriche di Pratolino* (Florence, 1742), esp. pp. 9, 21-22.

40. Moryson, *Itinerary*, pp. 327-28.

41. R. Strong, *The Renaissance Garden in England* (London, 1979), pp. 82-83.

42. Montaigne, *Journal*, pp. 186-89, 271-72.

43. W. Smith, "Pratolino," *Journal of the Society of Architectural Historians*, vol. 20, no. 4 (1961): 155-68.

44. Francesco de Vieri, *Delle maravigliose opere di Pratolino et d'amore* (Florence, 1586), pp. 43-44. This book perhaps was published in celebration of the villa's completion. See, too, C. Hülsen, 'Ein deutscher Architekt in Florenz (1600)," *Mitteilungen*, Kunsthistorisches Institut, Florence, vol. 7, no. 2 (1912): 152-93, esp. 167-69.

45. R. Gualterotti, *Vaghezza sopra Pratolino* (Florence, 1579), p. 10; and De Vieri, *Delle maravigliose*, p. 24. Both are cited by Smith, "Pratolino," pp. 164, 166.

46. J. Duncombe, *Letters from Italy in the Years 1754 and 1755* (London, 1773), p. 74.

47. De Vieri, *Delle maravigliose*, pp. 34-40, 42-44.

48. F. Baldinucci, *Notize de professori del disegno...1580 al 1610* (Florence, 1767-79), 2:497.

49. R. Strong, *Splendor at Court* (Boston, 1974), pp. 180, 195-96. In its use within the grotto, as within the theatre, the picture-frame stage epitomizes the late Renaissance world.

50. See Strong, *Splendor at Court*, p. 180.

51. B. de Rossi, *Descrizione dellapparato e degl'intermedi* (Florence, 1589).

52. Strong, *Splendor at Court*, p. 194.

53. See M. Calvesi, "Il sacro bosco di Bormarzo," in *Scritti di storia dell'arte in onore di Lionello Venturi* (Rome, 1960), 1:369-402. Heydenreich and Lotz, at the conclusion of their book, *Architecture in Italy*, pp. 325-26, note "the 'bizzarrie' [that] are the opposite of rule and order."

54. B. Gille, *Engineers of the Renaissance* (Cambridge, Mass., 1966), pp. 236-37.

55. R. Vaughan, *Philip the Good: The Apogee of Burgundy* (London, 1970), pp. 137-40.

56. See the preface in J. Androuet Du Cerceau the Elder, *Livre de grotesques* (Paris, 1566), which confirms that part of the ornamental designs are drawn from the decor of Fontainebleau. Also see the drawing, *Three-Bay Elevation and Circular Plan for a Grotto*, by John Webb after Serlio (bk. 3, p. 69; and bk. 4, p. 137), which is related to the Fontainebleau grotto, in J. Harris and A. Tait, *Catalogue of the Drawings by Inigo Jones, John Webb and Isaac De Caus at Worcester College* (Oxford, 1979), pp. 63-64.

57. N. Miller, "Domain of Illusion: The Grotto in France," in *"Fons Sapientiae,"* pp. 175-206.

58.. Cf. to a study for a bacchanalian feast attributed to Prospero Fontana, whose fresco of the same subject was begun in 1553 at the Villa Giulia. See J. Gere, "The Décor of the Villa Giulia," *Burlington Magazine*, 107 (1965): 198-206.

59. P. Faure, *Fonctions des cavernes crétoises* (Paris, 1964), p. 113.

60. J. Poldo d'Albenas, *Discours historial de l'antique et illustre cité de Nismes* (Lyon, 1560), pp. 84-87. See, too, L. Crema, *Enciclopedia classica*, vol. 12, tome 1, p. 466.

61. B. Andreas, *The Art of Rome* (New York, 1978), p. 591.

62. A. Blunt, *Philibert de l'Orme* (London, 1958), pp. 46-50, pls. 29, 32-34.

63. B. Palissy, *Recepte véritable, par laquelle tous les hommes de la France pourront apprendre à multiplier et augmenter leurs Thresors* (La Rochelle, 1563).

64. R. Josephon, *L'Architect de Charles XII: Nicodème Tessin à la cour de Louis XIV* (Paris and Brussels, 1930), p. 112.

65. E. Kris, "'Der Stil *Rustique*,' Die Verwendung des Naturabgusses bei Wenzel Jamnitzer und Bernard Palissy," *Jahrbuch der Kunsthistorischen Sammlungen in Wien*, 1 (1926): 207.

66. P. Rossi, *I philosofi e le macchine (1400-1700)* (Milan, 1962), pp. 11-24.

67. G. Bachelard, *The Poetics of Space*, trans. M. Jolas (Boston, 1969), pp. 127-32. See Battisti, *L'antirinascimento*, pp. 158-76.

68.. See N. Filleul, *Les Théatres de Gaillon* (Rouen, 1566), ed. F. Joukovsky (Paris, 1971), pp. 29, 33; also A.

Hulubei, *L'Eglogue en France au XVIe siècle* (Paris, 1938), pp. 498-501.

69. See Strong, *Splendor at Court,* pp. 151-52.

70. H. Couzy, "Le Château de Noisy- le- Roi," *La Revue de l'Art,* 38 (1977): 23-34. See, too, A. Mauban, *Jean Marot architecte et graveur parisien* (Paris, 1944), pp. 111, 310, n. 56.

71. Noisy manuscript (BN Imprimerie, Paris) FR 11651, "Suite Chronologique et historique des Seigneurs de Bailly et Noisy...depuis l'année 1720 jusqu'à présent," 1749, pp. 85-89.

72. For a contemporary description of the garden, see J. Odier, "Voyage en France d'un jeune homme morave en 1599 et 1600," *Mélanges d'archéologie et d'histoire publiés par l'Ecole française de Rome,* 43 (1926): f. 57v.

V. WORLDS OF FANCY: THE BAROQUE SPECTACLE

1. R. Descartes, *Traité du monde* (1629, published 1662), *Treatise of Man,* pt.2, trans. T. S. Hall (Cambridge, Mass., 1972), 21-22. Cf. *Oeuvres de Descartes,* ed. V. Cousin (Paris, 1824), 4:347-49.

2. Serlio's description [*Le premier (second) livre d'architecture* (Paris, 1545), bk. 2], of a satyric scene is according to Vitruvius, *De architectura* (5.6.9) replete with grotto and an appropriate cast; however, the accompanying woodcut is "domesticized" in its depiction of a northern landscape rather than scenography.

3. S. Orgel and R. Strong, *Inigo Jones: The Theatre of the Stuart Court,* 2 vols. (London and Berkeley, 1973).

4. See N. Sabbatini, *Pratica di fabricar scene e macchine ne' teatri* (Pesaro, 1638), bk. 2, chap. 5, pp. 74-75, cited in M. McGowan, *L'Art du ballet de cour en France, 1581-1643* (Paris, 1963), pp. 111-12. Cf. the variations on the grotto set into the stage of the theatre of Dionysus in Athens, as reconstructed in W. Jobst, *Die Höhle im Griechischen Theater des 5. und 4. Jahrunderts v. Christ,* Österreichische Akademie der Wissenschaften, vol. 26, no. 8, band 2 (Vienna, 1970): 141, fig. 2.

5. See, too, the drawing by Charles Errard, *A Deserted Landscape with Open Cave,* done in 1647 probably for the opera *Orphée,* in D. Onslager, *Stage Design* (New York, 1975), pp. 45-46.

6. T. E. Lawrenson, "La mise en scène dans *l'Arimène* de Nicolas de Montreux, "*Bibliothèque d'Humanisme et Renaissance,* 8 (1956): 286-90. See also G. Kernodle, *From Art to Theatre: Form and Convention in the Renaissance* (Chicago, 1943), p. 75.

7. L. de la Tourrasse, "Le Château-Neuf de Saint-Germain-en-Laye, ses terrasses et ses grottes, *Gazette des Beaux-Arts,* ser. 5, vol. 9 (1924): 68-95.

8. E. Soulié, ed., *Journal de Jean Héroard sur l'enfance et la jeunesse Louis XIII (1601-1628)* (Paris, 1868), 1:285, provides an account by the court doctor of the grottoes; these are also recorded in the engravings of Abraham Bosse, dating from circa 1625; and in A. Duchesne, *Les Antiquitez* [sic] *et recherches des villes, chasteaux et places plus remarquables de toute la France* (Paris, 1609), pp. 276-79.

9. For an excellent discussion of Salomon De Caus, see R. Strong, *The Renaissance Garden in England* (London, 1979), chap. 4, "The Mannerist Garden I," pp. 73-112. See C. S. Maks, *Salomon De Caus: 1576-1626* (Paris, 1935). De Caus's work is also prefigured in Jacques Besson's *Instrumentorum et machinarum liber primus* (Orleans, 1569?), p. 51, in which is depicted an aeolian and perpetual fountain with music-making devices.

10. S. De Caus, *Les Raisons des forces mouvantes avec diverses machines tant utiles que plaisantes* (Paris, 1624), *passim.* See A. Chapuis and E. Droz, *Les Automates, figures artificielles d'hommes et d'animaux* (Neuchâtel, 1949), pp. 35-38.

11. See Chapuis and Droz, *Automates,* pp 35-38 and 43-50, for a discussion of sixteenth- and seventeenth-century hydraulic automatons. See also L. Fehrle-Burger, *Die Welt der Oper in den Schlossgärten von Heidelberg und Schwetzingen* (Karlsruhe, 1977), pp. 37-50.

12. D. Hall, *The Book of Knowledge of Ingenious Mechanical Devices by Al-Jazari* (Dordrecht, 1974). See also B. Gille, *Engineers of the Renaissance* (Cambridge, Mass., 1966), pp. 23-81, 236-37.

13. See M. Charageat, *L'Art des jardins* (Paris, 1962), pp. 85-100.

14. Cf. E. Battisti, *L'antirinascimento* (Milan, 1962), pp. 238-43, nn. 454-55, "Per una iconologia degli automi." Also C. Hülsen, "Ein deutscher Architekt in Florenz (1600)," *Mitteilungen,* Kunsthistorisches Institut, Florence, vol. 7, no. 2 (1912): 152-93, esp. 166-69.

15. M. L. Gothein, *A History of Garden Art,* 2 vols., trans. Archer-Hind (London and New York, 1928), 2:40. A. Zeller, *Das Heidelberger Schloss: Werden, Zerfall und Zukunft* (Karlsruhe, 1905), pp. 69-71, figs. 79a-e.

16. Another edition was published in Paris in 1624. Here in Book 2 and in the *Hortus Palatinus,* De Caus describes and illustrates his inventions and grottoes in a manner reminiscent of Hero's when outlining his theorems. R. Patterson, "The 'Hortus Palatinus' at Heidelberg and the Reformation of the World. Part I: The Iconography of the Garden; Part II: Culture as Science," *Journal of Garden History,* 1 (1981): 1:67-104; 2:179-202, examines the meaning of the garden in cosmic terms, with particular reference to scientific, intellectual, and political currents of the time.

17. R. Strong, *The Renaissance Garden in England,* p.85.

18. Strong, *Renaissance Garden,* p. 103.

19. Isaac's treatise was translated into English by John Leak as *New and Rare Inventions of Waterworks Shewing the Easiest Waies to Raise Water Higher than the Spring* (London, 1659).

20. E. W. Griffith, ed., *Through England on a Side Saddle in the Time of William and Mary, Being the Diary of Celia Fiennes* (London, 1888), pp. 4-5.

21. J. Evelyn, *Diary from 1641 to 1705-6,* ed. W. Bray (London, 1889), 1:233. For Huygen's description of 1652, see Strong, *Renaissance Garden,* p. 156.

22. J. Woolridge, *Systema Horti-Culturae or The Art of Gardening, Describing the World of Late Renaissance*

Mechanical Marvels, 3rd ed. (London, 1688).

23. I. De Caus, *Wilton Garden (or Hortus Pembrochianus)* (London, ca. 1647), *View of Grotto*, pl. 20, no. 23. See C. Campbell, *Vitruvius Britanicus*, 5 vols. (London, 1717-1725), vol. 2, pl. 65.

24. I. De Caus, *New and Rare Inventions of Water-works*, trans. John Leak (London, 1659), pp. 20-21. Cited in Strong, *Renaissance Garden*, p. 156.

25. J. Summerson, *Art and Architecture in England: 1530-1830* (Harmondsworth, 1970), p. 148, notes that this grotto architecture probably relates to the erection about 1624 of a grotto by Isaac De Caus in the basement of Whitehall. See, too, P. Palme, *Triumph of Peace: A Study of the Whitehall Banqueting House* (Stockholm, 1956), pp. 66-67, for an account of a grotto/wine cellar as a place for diversion recorded in an entry in Pepys's diary dated May 29, 1664 [H. B. Wheatley, ed., *The Diary of Samuel Pepys* (London, 1903), 4:135].

26. *Woburn, Guide* (Norwich, 1977).

27. Ibid. See, too, B. Jones, *Follies and Grottoes* (London, 1974), pp. 145-46. The unique, though curious, style of this grotto prompts Strong (*Renaissance Garden*, pp. 139-41) to attribute three Victoria and Albert designs, dating from the 1620s to 1630s to Isaac De Caus.

28. E. Burton, *The Pageant of Stuart England* (New York, 1962), pp. 372-75.

29. R. Plot, *Natural History of Oxfordshire* (Oxford, 1677), pp. 236-39. See Strong, *Renaissance Garden*, pp. 130-33, who connects this grotto to the world of Renaissance hermeticism and to F. Bacon's *New Atlantis* of 1627.

30. Strong, *Renaissance Garden*, pp. 130-31.

31. S. De Caus, *Les Raisons*, bk. 2, p. ii. B. Woodcroft, ed., *The Pneumatics of Hero of Alexandria* (London, 1851), p. 68. See, too, E. MacDougall and N. Miller, *"Fons Sapientiae": Garden Fountains in Illustrated Books, Sixteenth-Eighteenth Centuries* (Washington, D.C., 1977).

32. F. Thompson, *A History of Chatsworth: Being a Supplement to the Sixth Duke of Devonshire's Handbook* (New York and London, 1979), p. 45.

33. Thompson, *History of Chatsworth*, pp. 44-45, 121-23, 224.

34. J. D. Hunt and P. Willis, *The Genius of the Place: The English Landscape Garden 1670-1820* (London, 1975), pp. 89-90.

35. H. Hibbard, *Carlo Maderno* (University Park, Pa., 1971), pp. 199-200.

36. R. Lanciana, *Wanderings in the Roman Campagna* (London, 1909), pp. 247-57, notes the continuity by pointing to the superposition of the Abbey of Grottaferrata onto the Tusculum of Cicero.

37. R. M. Steinberg, "The Iconography of the Teatro dell'Acqua at the Villa Aldobrandini," *Art Bulletin*, 47 (1965): 452-63.

38. Steinberg, "Iconography of the Teatro dell'Acqua," p. 462.

39. J. Evelyn, *Diary*, ed. E. S. De Beer, 6 vols. (Oxford, 1955), 2:392. See, too, G. Masson, *Italian Gardens* (London, 1966), pp. 191-92.

40. C. Franck, *The Villas of Frascati, 1550-1750* (London, 1956), p. 65.

41. R. Coope, *Salomon De Brosse* (London, 1972), pp. 132-33, pls. 173-75. See A. Mauban, *Jean Marot: Architecte et graveur parisien* (Paris, 1944), p. 162.

42. E. De Ganay, *Châteaux et manoirs de France: Ile-de-France* (Paris, 1939), 4:45-47, pls. 71-73, A. Marie, *Jardins français crées à la Renaissance* (Paris 1955), p. 36, figs. 210-16. Once attributed to Le Mercier, a recently published document supports the role of Francine: see "Devis et marché pour la construction de la grotte sur les dessins de Thomas Francine, 30 juillet 1635," in C. Grodecki, "La Construction du château de Wideville, " *Bulletin Monumentale*, vol. 136, no. 2 (1978): 135-75, esp. 151-56, 165-66.

43. N. Villa, *Le XVIIe Siècle vu par Abraham Bosse, graveur du roy* (Paris, 1967), p. 16, pl. 28.

44. J. Evelyn, *Diary, from 1641 to 1705-6*, ed. W. Bray (London, 1889), 1:58 (entry for 1644). See MacDougall and Miller, *"Fons Sapientiae,"* p. 64. According to W. H. Adams, *The French Garden* (New York, 1979), pp. 58-59, this was part of the search for an acceptable style for grottoes at the time. These are the grottoes that in 1661 inspired René Rapin's verses proclaiming the astonishing effects of the waterworks. See the quotes in Hunt and Willis, *Genius of the Place*, pp. 84-85: "Such diff'rent shapes, as great *Ruel* can boast,/ Where glorious *Richelieu* with excessive cost...." The grotto of Tanlay is surely part of this spectacle.

45. In this fragment and in Texte VIII, "Neptune à ses tritons," La Fontaine celebrates the grotto. J. de la Fontaine, *Le Songe de Vaux*, ed. E. Titcomb (Geneva and Paris, 1967), pp. 123-36, 205-11. Also P. A. Wadsworth, *Young La Fontaine* (Evanston, Ill., 1952).

46. See M. de Scudéry's description of the grotto in *Clélie*, cited in J. Cordey, *Vaux-le-Vicomte* (Paris, 1924), pp. 91ff.

47. For a description of the grotto in all its phases, see the excellent analysis by L. Châtelet-Lange, "La Grotte de Thetis et le premier Versailles de Louis XIV," *Art de France*, 1 (1961): 133-48. Also R. Pacciani, "'Heliaca.' Simbologia del sole nella politica culturale di Luigi XIV," *Psicon* 1 (1974): 74-78.

48. See Ch. Perrault, *Mémoires de ma vie* (Paris, 1684), ed. P. Bonnefon (Paris, 1909), p. 110.

49. Its triple-arch facade lacks the elegance of the sixteenth-century fountain house, the *Fontaine des Innocents*, and of its more prosaic immediate predecessor, the Reservoir of the Cloister of St. Germain l'Auxerrois built in 1607. See F. Boudon, A. Chastel, et al., *Système de l'architecture urbaine: Le quartier des Halles à Paris* (Paris, 1977), 1:325, fig. 418.

50. M. de Scudéry, *La Promenade de Versailles* (Paris, 1920).

51. J. de la Fontaine, *Amours de Psyché et de Cupidon*, ed. P. Clarac (Paris, 1942), pp. 128-31, nn. 822-23. See, too, *L'Églogue de Versailles, pastorale heroique représentée pour la première fois devant Sa Majesté . . . dans la GROTTE, à Versailles*, in *Recueil général des opera . . . ,* 16 vols. (Paris, 1703-45), tome 3.

52. Scudéry, *Promenade de Versailles*, pp. 42-47.

53. P. Verlet, *Versailles* (Paris, 1961), p. 138; P. De

Nolhac, *Les Jardins de Versailles* (Paris, 1906), pp. 79-80.

54. This was the spectacle of the *3ème journée* in the volume commemorating the festivities, *Les Divertissements de Versailles . . .* , engraved by A. LePautre and F. Chauveau (Paris, 1676).

55. J. de la Fontaine, *Amours,* cited in P. De Nolhac, *La Création de Versailles* (Paris, 1925), p. 131.

56. Verlet, *Versailles,* p. 79.

57. A. and J. Marie, *Versailles — son histoire.* Vol. 2. *Mansart à Versailles* (Paris, 1972), 2:505.

58. Marie, *Versailles,* pp. 505-07.

59. De Nolhac, *Les Jardins de Versailles,* pp. 108-09.

VI. SPLENDID IMPROPRIETIES: PICTURES IN A LANDSCAPE

1. O. Kürz, *"Huius Nympha Loci:* A Pseudo-Classical Description and a Drawing by Dürer," *Journal of the Warburg and Courtauld Institutes,* 16 (1953): 170-71.

2. For a definition of the picturesque, see J. Summerson, *Architecture in Britain, 1530-1830,* 5th rev. ed. (Harmondsworth, 1970), pp. 291-92, who discusses the change in meaning from its application to "the kind of landscape which recalled landscape painting" to the "real Picturesque," which begins circa 1794-95 in the works of R. P. Knight, U. Price, and H. Repton. For example, the latter maintained "that every estate had certain latent characteristics, which it was the aim of 'improvement' to elucidate and reinforce."

3. H. Walpole, *The History of Modern Taste in Gardening* (London, 1780); I. W. U. Chase, ed., *Horace Walpole: Gardenist* (Princeton, N. J., 1943), p. 134.

4. A. A. Cooper, 3rd Earl of Shaftesbury, *Characteristics,* 3 vols., *The Moralists: A Rhapsody* (London, 1711), 2:393.

5. Alexander Pope, "Epistle IV. To Richard Boyle, Earl of Burlington," in *Epistles to Several Persons (Moral Essays),* ed. F. W. Bateson (London and New Haven, 1961), pp. 142-43.

6. See C. Hussey, *The Picturesque* (London, 1927), p. 178. Also R. Morris on *Lectures on Architecture,* delivered in 1734 (London, 1759), cited in J. D. Hunt and P. Willis, *The Genius of the Place: The English Landscape Garden 1670-1820* (London, 1975), pp. 233-35, gives suggestions for "Little Fabricks [to be] erected in the Gardens of some *Noble Patron* of Arts: . . . Rills of Water . . . would create a kind of *melancholy musical Tone,* not altogether unpleasant." Further testimony to the genre's popularity in eighteenth-century England may be found in popular design manuals that supplied grotto trappings; see, for example, B. Langley, *The City and the Country Builder's and Workman's Treasury of Designs* (London, 1750), pl. 148, *Marble Tables for Grottoes,* dated 1739.

7. R. Chandler, *Travels in Asia Minor and Greece: An Account of a Tour (1765),* 2 vols., 3rd ed. (London, 1817), 1:66-67, 172-75, *passim.*

8. J. Evelyn, *Diary from 1641 to 1705-06,* ed. W. Bray, 4 vols. (London, 1879), 2:354. E. W. Mainwaring,

Italian Landscape in Eighteenth-Century England (New York, 1965), p. 122. Also R. A. Aubin, "Grottoes, Geology, and the Gothic Revival," *Studies in Philology,* 31 (1934): 408-16; and T. Burnett, *Theory of the Earth* (London, 1684), pp. 115-16. See, too, F. Bracher, "Pope's Grotto: The Maze of Fancy," *Huntington Library Quarterly,* vol. 12, n. 2 (1949): 141-62.

9. *The Victoria History of the Counties of England: Buckinghamshire* (London, 1925), 3:85, 136.

10. National Monuments Record, *High Wycombe (Buckinghamshire), Guide, Hell Fire Caves* (London, n.d.), pp. 1-7; also D. McCormick's popular account, *The Hell-Fire Club: The Story of the Amorous Knights of Wycombe* (London, 1975), pp. 43-45, 119-20, 168-71.

11. See the discussion of Stowe in N. Pevsner, *The Buildings of England: Buckinghamshire* (Harmondsworth, 1960), pp. 261-63.

12. These verses were written on the occasion of the publication of *The Designs of Inigo Jones, Consisting of Plans and Elevations for Public and Private Buildings* (London, 1727). See *Stowe, The Gardens of the Right Honorable Richard Lord Viscount Cobham,* addressed to Mr. Pope, including the essay, *Of False Taste,* to Richard Earl of Burlington (on the occasion of the publication of Palladio's Designs . . .) by Mr. Pope (London, 1732), p. 25.

13. Hunt and Willis, *Genius of the Place,* p. 215. Gilpin's first publication dealing with the picturesque was his *Dialogue upon the Gardens at Stowe,* published anonymously in 1748. Bridgeman did the grounds from 1725 on, Kent the Elysian Fields and the Grecian Valley. Cobham found the best architects for the garden buildings: Vanbrugh, Gibbs, and Kent. See L. Whistler, M. Gibson, G. Clarke, *Stowe: A Guide to the Gardens,* rev. ed. (Stowe, 1968).

14. R. Paulson, *Emblem and Expression: Meaning in English Art of the Eighteenth Century* (Cambridge, Mass., 1975), pp. 22-23.

15. H. F. Clark, *The English Landscape Garden* (London, 1948), p. 57.

16. Hunt and Willis, *Genius of the Place,* p. 245.

17. L. Whistler, M. Gibson, G. Clarke, *Guide to the Gardens,* p. 22.

18. See Virgil, *Aen.* 4.124-25: "To the same cave shall come Dido and the Trojan chief." See B. Seeley, *Stowe: A Description of the Magnificent House and Gardens of . . . Richard Grenville Temple, Earl Temple, Viscount and Baron Cobham* (London, 1769), p. 8, pl. 2; p. 18, pl. 4.

19. Seeley, *Stowe,* p. 28, pl. 6. Also B. Seeley, *Stowe: The Gardens of the Right Honorable Lord Viscount Cobham* (London, 1750), p. 12.

20. See J. Lees-Milne, *Earls of Creation* (London, 1962), pp. 140-48. Restoration on the grotto began in 1979.

21. R. Fedden and R. Joekes, eds., *The National Trust Guide to England, Wales and Northern Ireland,* rev. ed. (New York, 1977), pp. 239-40.

22. J. H. Pye, *A Peep into the Principal Seats and Gardens in and About Twickenham (The Residence of the Muses) . . . By a Lady of Distinction . . .* (London, 1775).

23. See Fedden and Joekes, *National Trust Guide to*

England, Wales and Northern Ireland, p. 239.

24. S. Johnson, *Lives of the English Poets,* ed. G. B. Hill, 3 vols. (Oxford, 1905), 3:135. See, too, B. Sprague Allen, *Tides in English Taste (1619-1800): A Background for the Study of Literature,* 2 vols. (New York, 1958), 2:133-35.
25. Bracher, "Pope's Grotto," pp. 141-62.
26. C. Thatcher, *Masters of the Grotto: Joseph and Josiah Lane* (Tisbury, 1976), p. 9.
27. Cf. C. Hussey, *English Gardens and Landscape: 1700-1750* (London, 1967), p. 43.
28. J. Searle, *A Plan of Mr. Pope's Garden* (London, 1745), p. 7.
29. See Bracher, "Pope's Garden," p. 107; M. Mack, *The Garden and the City. Retirement and Politics in the Later Poetry of Pope. 1731-1743* (Toronto, 1969), pp. 51, 56, 240.
30. G. Sherburn, ed., *The Correspondence of Alexander Pope,* 5 vols. (Oxford, 1956), 2:296.
31. Cited in Mack, *Garden and City,* p. 44.
32. Mack, *Garden and City,* p. 42, from the letter to E. Blount, June 2, 1725. H. F. Clark, "Eighteenth-Century Elysiums: The Role of 'Association' in the Landscape Movement," *Journal of the Warburg and Courtauld Institutes,* 6 (1943): 165-89, esp. 168.
33. Mack, *Garden and City,* p. 46.
34. Cited in Mack, *Garden and City,* pp. 46-47.
35. Ibid., p. 47.
36. A. Pope, *Odyssey* (1808), vol. 1. See bk. 5, pp. 71-83.
37. Mack, *Garden and City,* p. 61. See Johnson, *Lives of the English Poets,* 3:135.
38. See Mack, *Garden and City,* p. 67.
39. M. R. Brownell, *Alexander Pope and the Arts of Georgian England* (Oxford, 1979), pp. 254-71, esp. 267-70. The author also notes that Pope probably had read Borlase's description of a mine in Cornwall, visited ca. 1740.
40. Allen, *Tides in English Taste,* 2:133-35.
41. Mack, *Garden and City,* p. 60.
42. Ibid., p. 136. Also Mainwaring, *Italian Lanscape in Eighteenth-Century England,* p. 128, n. 13.
43. E. Malins, *English Landscaping and Literature* (London, 1966), pp. 104-05.
44. See R. M. Davis, "Stephen Duck, The Thresher-Poet," *University of Maine Studies,* 2nd ser., no. 8 (1926): 1-198, esp. 72.
45. Cited in Davis, "Stephen Duck," p. 75.
46. Davis, "Stephen Duck," p. 77.
47. Kürz, "Huius Nympha loci," pp. 171-77. The setting of the Stourhead nymph harks back to that of the reclining "Ariadne" set up in the Belvedere statue court in 1512; see E. MacDougall, "The Sleeping Nymph: Origins of a Humanist Fountain Type," *Art Bulletin,* 57 (1975): 357-65, esp. fig. 1, the drawing by Francesco de Hollanda, 1538-39.
48. K. Woodbridge, *Landscape and Antiquity: Aspects of English Culture at Stourhead, 1718 to 1835* (Oxford, 1970), *passim.* Hussey, *English Gardens and Landscapes,* p. 162.
49. P. Toynbee, ed., *Horace Walpole's Journals of Visits to Country Seats,* vol. 16, Walpole Society (Oxford, 1928), p. 43; and J. Turner, "The Structure of Henry Hoare's Stourhead," *Art Bulletin,* 61 (1979): 68-77.
50. Paulson, *Emblem and Expression,* pp. 26ff; C. Hussey, "The Gardens at Stourhead, Wilts," *Country Life,* 83, June 11, 1938, pp. 608-14. Woodbridge, *Landscape and Antiquity,* p. 31.
51. R. C. Hoare, *Description of the House and Gardens at Stourhead,* rev. ed. (Bath, 1818), pp. 23-24. Cf. *Aeneid* 1.167-68: "Inside are sweet waters and seats of living rock—the house of the nymphs."
52. Hussey, *English Gardens and Landscapes,* p. 162.
53. J. Britton, *The Beauties of Wiltshire,* 3 vols. (London, 1801-37), 2:15-16.
54. O. Sirén, *China and the Gardens of Europe of the Eighteenth Century* (New York, 1950), pp. 48-49, pls. 48-53, *passim.*
55. Thatcher, *Masters of the Grotto,* pp. 10-11, 15.
56. Sirén, *China and the Gardens of Europe,* pp. 3-12.
57. A. O. Lovejoy, "The Chinese Origin of a Romanticism," in *Essays in the History of Ideas* (Baltimore and London, 1948), p. 129.
58. See Thatcher, *Masters of the Grotto,* p. 13.
59. E. Burke, *A Philosophical Inquiry into the Origin of Our Ideas of the Sublime and Beautiful* (1757; New York, 1909), pp. 64, 70, 71.
60. See Thatcher, *Masters of the Grotto,* pp. 23-28, citing Beckford's satirical *Modern Novel Writing or The Elegant Enthusiast.*
61. Ibid., pp. 15-20.
62. M. Whiffen, "Vandalism Triumphant: The Destruction of Oatlands Grotto," *Architectural Review,* vol. 103, no. 617 (May 1948): 216-18.
63. Ibid.; R. Strong, M. Binney, and J. Harris, *The Destruction of the Country House: 1875-1975* (London, 1974), pl. 320.
64. M. Jourdain, "Shellwork Rooms and Grottoes," *Country Life,* 95 (February 1944): pp. 241-43.
65. B. Howe, "A Shell Grotto Restored," *Country Life,* 125, June 4, 1959, p. 1252.
66. Cited in Jourdain, "Shellwork Rooms and Grottoes," p. 241.
67. Ibid., pp. 241-43; also *Country Life,* 73, July 9 and 16, 1932.
68. Jourdain, "Shellwork Rooms and Grottoes," p. 241. See, too, J. Wesley, *Journal* (London, 1788), cited by A. Oswald, "Goldney House, Clifton-II," *Country Life,* 104 (August 1948): 328-31.
69. Thatcher, *Masters of the Grotto,* pp. 20-21. See, too, Howe, "Shell Grotto Restored," p. 252.
70. Letter, N. M. Woodall, "The Art of the Grotto," *Country Life,* 133, June 6, 1963, p. 1328.
71. Cf. Bracher, "Pope's Grotto."
72. W. Shenstone, *Works,* 2 vols. (London, 1764), 2: 367-68. See also J. Riely, 'Shenstone's Walks: The Genesis of the Leasowes," *Apollo,* 110 (1979): 205, fig. 5.
73. W. H. Adams, "Thomas Jefferson and the Art of the Garden," *Apollo,* 104 (1976): 190-97.
74. See R. Girardin, *De la Composition des paysages* (Paris, 1805), p. 94.
75. E. De Ganay, *Beaux Jardins de France* (Paris, 1950), pp. 131-41. Also C. Samaran, *Paysages littéraires du Valois de Rousseau à Nerval* (Paris, 1964), pp. 64-65.
76. R. L. Girardin, *Promenade ou itinéraire des jardins d'Ermenonville...* (Paris, 1788), p. 16. (The book includes twenty-four etchings by J. Mérigot.) R.

Girardin, *De la Composition des paysages* (Paris, 1777), pp. 16-17.

77. J. J. Rousseau, *La Nouvelle Héloïse*, ed. D. Mornet, 4 vols. (Paris, 1925), 3:225-35; cited in M. B. Ellis, *La Nouvelle Héloïse: A Synthesis of Rousseau's Thought* (Toronto, 1949), pp. 92-93. See P. Willis, "Rousseau, Stow and le Jardin Anglais," *Studies on Voltaire and the Eighteenth Century*, 40 (1972): 1791-98, esp. 1792.

78. A. L. J. de Laborde, *Description des nouveaux jardins de France et ses anciens châteaux* (Paris, 1808-25), pp. 60-61; W. H. Adams, *The French Garden. 1500-1800* (New York, 1979), pp. 119-20; O. Sirén, "Le Désert de Retz," *Architectural Review*, 106 (November 1949): 327-32.

79. [R.L. Girardin], *Promenades ou itinéraire des jardins de Chantilly* (Paris, 1791), pp. 33-34.

80. G. Grigson, "The Origin of Grottoes," *Country Life*, 108, September 1, 1950, pp. 688-93. G. L. Le Rouge, *Jardins à la mode et jardins anglo-chinois*, ed. D. Jacomet, 18 cahiers (1776; Paris, 1878); many plates are copied after other publications. The enthusiasm of Westerners for the virtues of Chinese civilization soon led to the idea of "beauty without order" as supposedly realized in Chinese gardens. This was first expressed in England by Sir William Temple in his essay, "Upon the Gardens of Epicurus," [*The Works,* 2 vols. (London, 1731), vol. 1] wherein he extols the more subtle beauty of the irregular.

81. H. Honour, *Chinoiserie: The Vision of Cathay* (New York, 1961), pp. 164-65.

82. E. Kaufmann, *Architecture in the Age of Reason* (New York, 1965), pp. 182, 202, 204, 208.

83. J. Langner, "Architecture pastorale sous Louis XVI," *Art de France*, 3 (1963): 170-86.

84. Ibid.; also p. 185. See the *laiterie*-grotto at Méréville with its bathing Diane lit from above in L. Laborde, *Description des nouveaux jardins de France* (Paris, 1809), p. 104, pl. 50.

85. J. F. de Neufforge, *Recueil élémentaire d'architecture*, 8 vols., 2 supps. (Paris, 1757-77); Kaufmann, *Architecture in the Age of Reason*, p. 151ff.

86. See De Ganay, *Beaux Jardins de France*, pp. 149-50.

87. Caisse Nationale des Monuments Historiques et des Sites, *Jardins en France 1760-1820. Pays d'illusion, terre d'expériences* (Paris, 1977). J. Catinat, *Les Châteaux de Chatou et le nymphée de Soufflot* (Paris, 1974), chap. 5, esp. pp. 52, 55.

88. M. Raval and J. C. Moreaux, *Claude-Nicolas Ledoux: 1756-1806* (Paris, 1946), pp. 50-51, 60-61, *passim.*

89. Y. Christ, *Projects et divagations de Claude-Nicolas Ledoux: Architecte du Roi* (Paris, 1961), pp. 13-14. Ledoux's classicism is also expressed in the small Palladian Château of Eguière, which is entwined with a grotto.

90. J. Stern, *A l'Ombre de Sophie Arnould. François Joseph Belanger, architecte des Menus Plaisirs . . .*, 2 vols. (Paris, 1930), 1:140-41. Also Sirén, *China and the Gardens of Europe*, pp. 148-52; Adams, *French Garden*, pp. 125-26.

91. For an excellent discussion of the "organic power of nature" and the "new geometric order," see R.

Rosenblum, *Transformations in Late Eighteenth Century Art* (Princeton, N.J., 1967), esp. pp. 118-23.

92. See N. Pevsner, *An Outline of European Architecture* (Harmondsworth, 1974), pp. 371-72.

93. Raval and Moreaux, *Ledoux*, pp. 60-61.

94. C. N. Ledoux, *L'Architecture considerée sous le rapport de l'art, des moeurs et de la législation*, 2 vols. (Paris, 1804), vol. 1; also *L'Architecture de C. N. Ledoux*, 2 vols. (Paris, 1842).

95. Kaufmann, *Architecture in the Age of Reason*, p. 165.

96. See Lequeu's "Subterranean Labyrinth for a Gothic House," in J. C. Lemagny, *Visionary Architects: Boullée, Ledoux, Lequeu* (Houston, Tex., 1968), pp. 186-87. See, too, A. Vidler, "The Architecture of Lodges: Ritual Form and Associational Life in the Late Enlightenment," *Oppositions*, 5 (Summer 1976): 75-97.

97. N. Pevsner, *Studies in Art, Architecture and Design*, 2 vols. (London, 1968), 1:183, fig. 17.

98. J.-J. Lequeu, *Architecture civile*, Cabinet des Estampes, Bibliothèque Nationale (Paris, 1793), vol. 1, pt. 2, figs. 98-99, 138.

99. Cf. Lequeu's *Grote Oceanitides* (sic) to Inigo Jones's *House of Oceanus* for Ben Jonson's masque, *The Fortunate Isles and Their Union*, in S. Orgel and R. Strong, *Inigo Jones: The Theatre of the Stuart Court*, 2 vols. (London and Berkeley), 1:376-78.

100. M. l'abbé Delille, trans., *Les Jardins ou l'art d'embellir les paysages* (Paris, 1782), chap. 4, 88ff.

101. Ville de Paris, *Grandes et petites heures du Parc Monceau*, Musée Cernuschi (Paris, 1981), pp. 42, 50; Adams, *French Garden*, pp. 118-19.

102. J. A. LeRoi, *Histoire de Versailles . . . de cette ville jusqu'à nos jours*, 2 vols. (Versailles, 1868), 1:377ff.

103. G. Desjardins, *Le Petit-Trianon, histoire et description* (Versailles, 1885), pp. 196-97, 346-47.

VII. ECLECTIC ABERRATIONS: SWAN SONG

1. See M. L. Gothein, *A History of Garden Art*, trans., Archer-Hind, 2 vols. (London and Toronto, 1928), 2:125-28. Designed by an architect of the school of Le Nôtre, the Great Garden at Herrenhausen combined the French garden with schemes derived from the Dutch.

2. N. Pevsner, *An Outline of European Architecture* (Harmondsworth, 1974), pp. 263-87, esp. p. 286.

3. J. Furtenbach, *Architectura recreationis* (Augsburg, 1640), pls. 24, 25, 28. Gothein, *History of Garden Art*, 2:9-10.

4. F. Lugt and J. Vallery-Radot, *Inventaire général des dessins des écoles du Nord* (Paris, 1936), pp. 22-24.

5. E. Berckenhagen, *Deutsche Garten vor 1800* (Hanover and Berlin, 1962), pp. 10-11; H. Kreisel and H. Thoma, *Residenz München* (Munich, 1937), pp. 36-37, fig. 6.

6. For Wilhelmshöhe, see F. Lometsch, *Wilhelmshöhe* (Kassel, 1961); P. O. Rave, *Garten der Barockzeit* (Stuttgart, 1951); A. Hoffmann, *Park Wilhelmshöhe*, Guide Kassel (Kassel, n.d.); Gothein, *History of Garden Art*, 2:128-31.

7. G. F. Guerneiro, *Delineatio montis* (Rome, 1705), Kassel, 1706). See Staatliche Museen zu Berlin, Katalog der Ornamentstich, *Sammlung der Staatlichen Kunstbibliothek, Berlin* (New York, 1939), 2:425, for entries on Guernerio (nos. 3319-20). Also A. Holtmeyer, "Giovanni Francesco Guerneiro," *Zeitschrift für Geschichte der Architektur*, vol. 3, no. 2 (August 1910): 249-57.

8. H. Biehn, *Park Wilhelmshöhe:* (Kassel, n.d.). G. Lippold-Hälssig, *Deutsche Garten* (Dresden, 1958).

9. O. Zenkner, *Schwetzingen: Baroque Jewel of the Palatinate),* trans. E. Herbster (Schwetzingen, 1975), p. 20, *passim*. See "Schwetzingen" (folio of ten aquatints after drawings by C. Kunst), Bibliothèque Nationale, Cabinet des Estampes (Paris, n.d.).

10. Zenkner, *Schwetzingen*, p. 19.

11. Zenkner, *Schwetzingen*, p. 21.

12. W. Wenzel, *Die Garten des Lothar Franz von Schönborn: 1655-1729* (Berlin, 1970); Gothein, *History of Garden Art*, 2:146, 149.

13. S. Kleiner, *Représentation au naturel des châteaux de Weissenstein au dessus de Pommersfeld, et de celui de Geubach appartenant à la maison des Contes de Schönborn avec les jardins, les écuries...* (Augsburg, 1728). See Wenzel, *Garten des Lothar Franz von Schönborn*, pp. 28-29, figs. 16-19.

14. Gothein, *History of Garden Art.* 2:149.

15. H. Kreisel, *Das Schloss zu Pommersfelden* (Munich, 1953), pp. 53-55, figs. 60-61. M. H. von Freeden, *Pommersfelden: Schloss* (Königstein/Taunus, n.d.). See W. J. Hofmann, *Schloss Pommersfelden; Geschichte seiner Entstehung* (Nuremberg, 1968), pp. 151-55, figs. 62-63, on the *sala terrena*. Stuccoed in 1715 by Daniel Schenk, the grotto was vaulted by Johann Dientzenhofer, and the *rocaille* was added by George Hennick a few years later.

16. E. Herget, "Die Sala Terrena im deutschen Barock, unter besonderer Berüchsichtigung ihrer Entwicklung aus der abenlandischer Grottenarchitektur" (Ph.D. dissertation, University of Frankfurt, 1954).
    For Braunschweig, see U. von Alvensleben, *Die Braunschweigischen Schlösser der Barockzeit und ihr Baumeister Hermann Korb* (Berlin, 1937), pp. 22-23, fig. 3; also 28-29, figs. 6-7, for a discussion of Parnassus, a grand theatre in the rustic style. See, too, P. Decker, *Fürstlicher Baumeister, oder Architectura Civilis...*, 2 vols. (Augsburg, 1711-16); G. Gerkens, *Das Fürstliche Lustschloss Salzdahlum und sein Erbauer Herzog Anton Ulrich von Braunschweig-Wolfenbüttel* (Braunschweig, 1974), pp. 80-81, fig. 21, discusses the hierarchical scheme of a didactic statement in praise of Duke Anton Ulrich, the builder, wherein the subterranean grotto is interpreted as the abode of the nature gods and chthonic divinities.

17. H. Heckmann, *Matthäus Daniel Pöppelmann: Leben und Werk* (Berlin, 1972), pp. 132-35; H.G. Ermisch, *Der Dresdner Zwinger* (Dresden, 1956).

18. Pevsner, *Outline of European Architecture*, pp. 274-76, crisply encapsulates the spirit of rococo architecture.

19. Gothein, *History of Garden Art*, 2:178-79. See P. Hainhofer, *Des Ausburger Patriciers: Correspondenzen aus dem Jahren 1610-1619* (Vienna, 1894), p. 139, entry for 1611; Gothein, *History of Garden Art*, 2:31-34.

20. E. Bachmann, *The Hermitage at Bayreuth*, trans. B. Waldstein-Wartenberg (Munich, 1968). Gothein, *History of Garden Art*, 2:194-96.

21. C. Arthaud, *Dream Palaces: Fantastic Houses and Their Treasures* (London, 1973). See L. Hager, *Nymphenburg; Schloss, Park und Burgen* (Munich, 1955), pp. 40-43, for a hermitage-grotto devoted to the religious practices of the court hermit. Built in 1725, the Church of the Magdalene at Nymphenburg harbors a grotto-chapel. Water springing from its rocks was deemed miraculous by the populace.

22. E. Bachmann, *Neues Schloss Bayreuth* (Munich, 1972), pp. 62-63.

23. E. Bachmann, "Anfänge des Landschaftsgartens in Deutschland," *Zeitschrift für Kunstwissenschaft*, vol. 5, nos. 1-2 (1951): 203-28. See F. Fénelon, *Die seltsame Begebenheiten des Telemach* (Frankfurt and Leipzig, 1741), bk. 18, pp. 622-23, in which Telemachus descends into Hades. Also D. Hennebo and A. Hoffmann, *Der Architektonische Garten*, 2 vols. (Hamburg, 1965), 2: fig. 122.

24. J.B. Fischer von Erlach, *Entwurff einer historischen Architectur* (Leipzig, 1725), bk. II, pl. xiv, p.22. Also Gothein, *History of Garden Art*, 2:29. R. Meyer, *Hecken-und-Garten-theatre in Deutschland im 17. und 18. Jahrhundert* (Emsdetten, 1934), pp. 230-31, figs. 83-87.

25. Arthaud, *Dream Palaces*, pp. 153-56.

26. Gothein, *History of Garden Art*, 2:190-92. B. Meier, *Potsdam: Palaces and Gardens* (Berlin, 1930). W. Kurth, *Sanssouci: Ein Beitrag zur Kunst des Deutschen Rokoko* (Berlin, 1962), pp. 215-18, figs. 155-58. For the Grottensaal in the New Palace, see G. Piltz, *Sanssouci: Schlösser und Garten* (Dresden, 1954), p. 51.

27. H. Kreisel, *Der Rokokogarten zu Veitschöchheim* (Munich , 1953). Ibid., see figs. 12-13 for the Parnassus grotto by Ferdinand Tietz constructed between 1765-66. Also W. Tunk, *Veitshöchheim: Schloss und Garten* (Munich, 1977).

28. E. M. Neumeyer, "Landscape Garden in Rousseau, Goethe, Flaubert," *Journal of the History of Ideas,* 8 (1947): 187-217. For Wilhelmsthal, see H. W. Hegemann, *Burgen und Schlösser in Hessen* (Hanau, 1971), pp. 233-34; and H. Biehn, "Zwei bisher unbekannte Federzeichnungen der Grotte und der Warte in Schlosspark Wilhelmsthal," in *Schloss Charlottenberg, Berlin. Preussen, Festschrift für Margarete Kühn* (Berlin, 1975), pp. 307-12.

29. W. Huschke, *Die Geschichte des Parkes von Weimar* (Weimar, 1951), pp. 66-67; W. Vulpius, *Der Goethepark in Weimar* (Weimar, 1957), pp. 29-31; P.O. Rave, *Garten der Goethezeit* (Leipzig, 1941), p. 59, also fig. 8.

30. For the grottoes of Ludwig II of Bavaria, see D. and M. Petzet, *Die Richard Wagner-Bühne König Ludwigs II* (Munich, 1970), pp. 140-44, figs. 169-76, 248-63, pl. 8. See, too, A. Drigel, *König Ludwig II und die Kunst* (Munich, 1968), pp. 36-37; also ibid., illus. 38-39, cat. 893-95; S. Russ, *Bayerische Königsschlösser: Linderhof, Neuschwanstein, Herrenchiemsee* (Munich, 1977), pp. 46-47.

31. M. Petzet and G. Hojer, *Schloss Linderhof* (Munich,

1976); Arthaud, *Dream Palaces,* pp. 49-60. W. Blunt, *The Dream King: 1845-1886* (London, 1970), pp. 141, 146, 151-52, 232-34; H. Kreisel, *Die Schlösser Ludwigs II von Bayern* (Darmstadt, 1954), pp. 40-41.

32. M. Petzet and G. Hojer, *The Castle of Neuschwanstein* (Munich, 1977), p. 29.

33. F. W. von Goethe, *Elective Affinities,* trans. E. Mayer and L. Bogan (Chicago, 1963), pt. II, chap. 8. Neumeyer, "Landscape Garden," p. 206.

34. E. H. Gombrich, *The Sense of Order: A Study in the Psychology of Decorative Art* (Ithaca, N.Y., 1979), pp. 30-31. Also E. Kris, " 'Der Stil *Rustique,*' Die Verwendung des Naturabgusses bei Wenzel Jamnitzer und Bernard Palissy," *Jahrbuch der Kunsthistorischen Sammlungen in Wien,* Neue Folge, Band 1 (1926): 206.

VIII. EPILOGUE:
THE ARCHITECTURE OF ILLUSION

1. E. M. Neumeyer, "Landscape Garden in Rousseau, Goethe, Flaubert," *Journal of the History of Ideas,* 8 (1947): 216-17.

2. See, for example, F. L. Olmsted's spring grotto, built in the park on Capitol Hill, Washington, D.C., between 1874-75 as a cool retreat and as part of the landscaping program of the entire area.

3. C. J. Jung, *The Symbolic Life: Miscellaneous Writings* (Princeton, N.J., 1950), pp. 116-17; also pp. 38, 120, 123; idem, *Alchemical Studies* (London, 1967), pp. 101-04.

4. G. Bachelard, *La Poétique de l'espace* (Paris, 1957), chap. 1; trans. M. Jolas, *The Poetics of Space* (Boston, 1964) pp. 3-37. See, too, H. Stierlin, "L'Architecture souterraine," *Werk/Oeuvre,* 10 (October 1975): 879-912.

5. J. R. G. Hassard, "An American Museum of Art: The Designs Submitted by Wm. H. Beard," *Scribner's Monthly* (August 1871): 409-15; also "Wm. H. Beard, An American Museum of Art—1873," in *Unbuilt America: Forgotten Architecture in the United States . . . ,* eds. A. Sky and M. Stone, (New York, 1976), figs. 34-36.

6. Hassard, "An American Museum,"p. 413.

7. "Johnson Underground" in "Going Underground," *Progressive Architecture* 48 (April 1967): 146; also pp. 138-51.

8. J. Utzon, "The Silkeborg Museum," *Zodiac,* 14 (1965): 87-89.

9. M. Wells, "Why I Went Underground," *The Futurist* (February 1976): 21-24.

10. Military structures, bomb and nuclear shelters, and defense bunkers have reached a high degree of sophistication, exemplified in the underground citadel NORAD, the Combat Operations Center of the North American Air Defense Command in Colorado Springs. To date the range of building underground astonishes. The mammoth world of the Brunson Instrument Company in Kansas City is housed in a limestone cave 600 feet below the earth's surface to keep vibrations at a minimum, a condition vital for the manufacturing of high-precision optical instruments to be used on the moon. See, too, the natural rocklike cavity of Stockholm's sub-

way station in B. Jansson, "Terraspace—A World to Explore," *Underground Space,* 1 (1976-77): 9, 16-17.

11. G. Nelson, "The Hidden City," *Architecture Plus* 2 (November-December 1974): 70-77, considers "a new approach to end visual boredom in our cities" by making them less visible. See G. Bickerts, "Subterranean Systems: A Framework for a New Planning Policy," *The Architectural Forum,* 135 (November 1971): 58-59. Above all, the principal attraction of this subterranean world today is the possibility it offers for the conservation of energy and for climate control. Seasonal variations are eliminated, while the temperature and humidity are relatively constant. Note, too, the increasing frequency of such reports as "Bright Future Is Seen in Underground Development," *The New York Times,* June 12, 1981; a conference held in Kansas City, Mo., sponsored by the American Underground Space Association, based in Minneapolis, stressed reduction in energy consumption, pollution, and traffic congestion.

12. See *Underground Space,* 1 (1976), the official Journal of the American Underground Association (Oxford, Eng., and Elmsford, N.Y.).

13. See S. Kostof, *Caves of God. The Monastic Environment of Byzantine Cappadocia* (Cambridge, Mass., 1972).

14. U. Conrads, *Fantasy in Architecture,* (New York, 1963) p. 13.

15. Ibid., pp. 13, 62-63, 68.

16. See "Big Corporations Take Cover," *Progressive Architecture,* 48 (April 1967): 142. Cf. R. Sommer, *Tight Spaces. Hard Architecture and How to Humanize It* (Englewood Cliffs, N.J., 1974), pp. 115-16.

17. F. Kiesler, "The Future: Notes on Architecture as Sculpture," *Art in America,* 54 (May-June 1966): 57-68. Also, F.J. Kiesler, *Frederick Kiesler, Architekt: 1890-1965* (Vienna, 1975); F. Kiesler, "The Grotto for Meditation," *Craft Horizons,* no. 4 (July-August 1966): 22-27; and Frederick Kiesler, "Grotto for Meditation," from a tape made at New Harmony, Indiana, October 1964, in "Frederick Kiesler, 1923-1964," *Zodiac,* 19 (1969): 19-49, esp. 46-48.

18. H. Khunrath, *Amphitheatrum Sapientiae Aeternae* (Hanover, 1602). Cf., too, P. de l'Orme, *Le Premier Tôme de l'architecture* (1567; Paris, 1648), pp. 50-51, bk. 3, Prologue, where the architect, a man of wisdom and learning, emerges from the obscure cave, a place of contemplation, solitude, and study, having attained the true knowledge and perfection of his art through his sojourn there. We might also look to the dark irrational side of man as depicted by F. Dostoyevsky, *Notes from Underground,* trans. C. Garnett (New York, 1960). Here the metaphor of the underground is equated with a vision of human bondage. To Dostoyevsky, the will of man may be in direct conflict with the forces of reason; the good is not necessarily identified with the true. See M. C. Beardsley, "Dostoyevsky's Metaphor of the 'Underground,' " *Journal of the History of Ideas,* 3 (June 1942): 265-90.

19. Cited in Porphyry, *De Antro,* 8. Ultimately, the reader returns to Plato's allegory (*Rep.*7.514ff), wherein the passage of life is compared to the sojourn in a natural cavern.

Bibliographical Note

The literature that bears upon the grotto is almost infinite. Hence, I shall cite here only those sources that are central to the theme pursued. More detailed bibliographical information is given in the footnotes. N. Neuerburg's seminal publication on Roman nymphaea, *L'architettura delle fontane e dei ninfei nell'Italia antica*, Memorie dell'Accademia di Archeologia, Lettere e Belle Arti di Napoli, no. 5 (Naples, 1965), has spawned studies on specific monuments. E. Kris's " 'Der Stil *Rustique*, ' Die Verwendung des Naturabgusses bei Wenzel Jamnitzer und Bernard Palissy," *Jahrbuch der Kunsthistorischen Sammlungen in Wien,* Neue Folge, Band 1 (1926): 137-208, is still probably the most basic work for the Renaissance grotto; it explores the antithesis of nature and the art of antiquity as manifested in the sixteenth-century grotto and in the poetry of the Pléiade. For Italian grottoes, see especially B. Wiles's pioneering book, *The Fountains of the Florentine Sculptors and Their Followers* (Cambridge, Mass., 1933); E. B. MacDougall's investigations of Italian Renaissance fountains; D. Heikamp's attempt to define the nature of the grotto; and D. Coffin's key reference, *The Villa in the Life of Renaissance Rome* (Princeton, N.J., 1979). For French grottoes, see L. Châtelet-Lange's penetrating analyses in articles cited in the footnotes. Interpretative studies drawn upon include M. Mack's erudite depiction of Pope's grotto as an accessory to his muse in *The Garden and the City: Retirement and Politics in the Late Poetry of Pope, 1731-1734* (Toronto, 1969); and R. Strong's brilliant discussion of the grotto in *The Renaissance Garden in England* (London, 1979). A significant book is P. Saintyves, *Les Grottes dans les cultes magico-religieux et la symbolique primitive* (Paris, 1918), which includes a translation by J. Trabucco of Porphyry's *De Antro Nympharum*. No general history of garden art has yet superseded M. L. Gothein, *A History of Garden Art*, trans. Archer-Hind, 2 vols. (London, 1928). That the field is embarking on a new era is apparent in the publication of the *Journal of Garden History: An International Quarterly*, born in 1981. According to John Dixon Hunt, editor, its aim is to provide "a regular forum in which the full potential of the subject may discover itself" (p.1).

Sources of Illustrations

Grateful acknowledgement is made to the following sources who have kindly allowed permission to reproduce the following illustrations.

137

Index